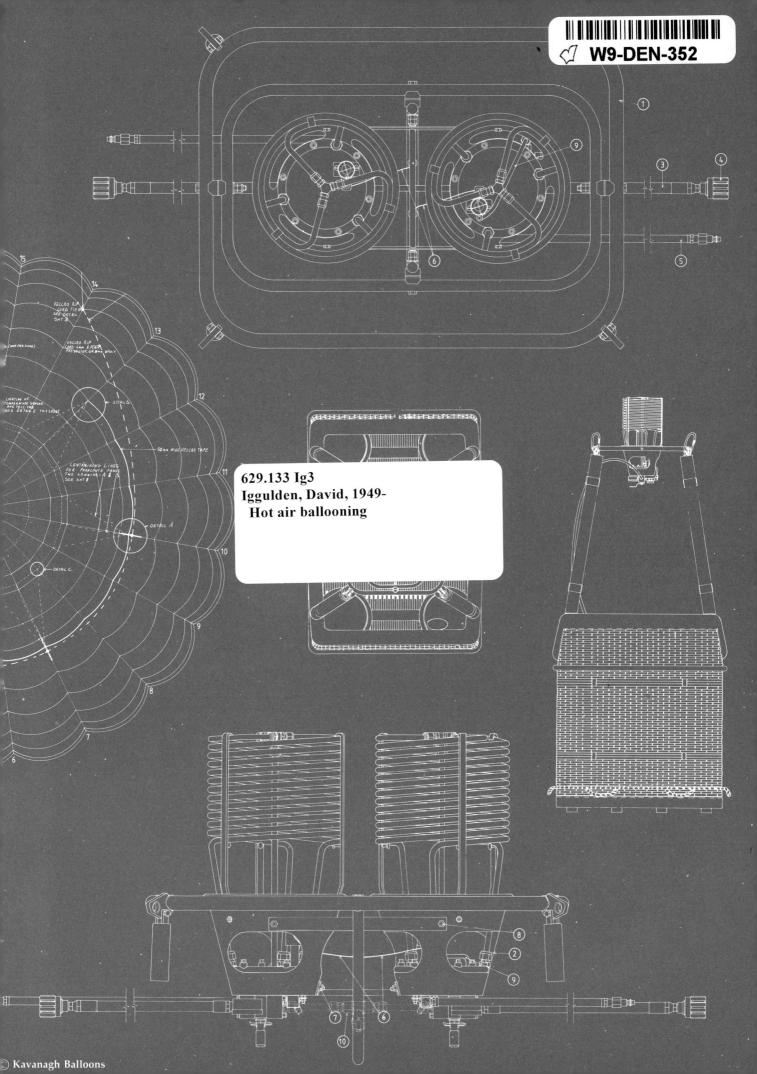

HOT AIR BALLOONING

HOT AIR

FOREWORD BY
RICHARD BRANSON AND PER LINDSTRAND

DAVID IGGULDEN

BALLOONING

Special thanks to photographer Sally Samins

Produced in Australia by Pierson & Co
PO Box 87 Mosman 2088
Tel: (02) 969 6521 Fax: (02) 969 6574

**National Library of Australia
Cataloguing-in-Publication Data:**

Iggulden, David, 1949-
Hot air ballooning.
Bibliography
ISBN 0 947068 12 0

1. Balloon ascensions. 2. Balloonists.
3. Hot air balloons. I. Title

797.51

Editor: Margot Lanagan
Designer: Diane Quick
Typesetter: Bookset
Printed in Singapore through GlobalCom

Page 1 Dr G. Michael Wall; page 2 Sally Samins; this page Dany Cleyet-Marrel;
page 5 (clockwise from top left) Sally Samins; Jerry Young/Katz Eyes; Bob Barbarick; Sally Samins;
Jerry Young/Katz Eyes; Thom Roberts Page 6 David Partridge/Air 2 Air Page 8 Balloon Aloft

CONTENTS

Acknowledgements   7

Foreword by Richard Branson
and Per Lindstrand   9

Chapter 1
Mad, Mad Balloonists   11

Chapter 2
The Bicentennial Decade   43

Chapter 3
On the Wind and a Prayer   91

Chapter 4
The Record Breakers   113

Chapter 5
Towards 2000   145

The modern Hot Air Balloon
by Per Lindstrand   167

International Competition
Tasks   170

Bibliography   173
Glossary   175

ACKNOWLEDGEMENTS

THE AUTHOR wishes to gratefully acknowledge the assistance, guidance and time given by many people in the preparation of this book. Without their help it would have been only gas and hot air. They are, in alphabetical order:

Louis Abruzzo, Airship Industries, Rocky Aoki, Balloon Sunrise, Mike Bradley, British Airways, Cameron Balloons, Canson & Montgolfier Paper, Cathay Pacific Airways, Phil Castleton, Dany Cleyet-Marrel, CNES Toulouse, Jean-Robert Cornuel, Peter Counsell, Hélène Dorigny, Phil Dunnington, Whiz Gambier, Global Concern, Geoff Green, Robin Higgs, Sabu Ichiyoshi, ICI Australia, Rien Jurg, Phil Kavanagh, Kavanagh Balloons, Joe Kittinger, Kodak Australasia, Dominic Michealis, Julie Molloy, Tim Molloy, Steve Moss, Museum of Transport and Technology of Auckland, the National Geographic Society, Alan Noble, John Owen, David Partridge and Air 2 Air, Nigel Pogmore, the Royal Aeronautical Society, Brenda Speirs, Thunder & Colt Balloons, Ian Tooth, Peter Vizzard, Aden Wickes, Ruth Wilson, Mary Woodhouse, Jim Woodman, Jerry Young and Robert Zirpolo.

Special thanks to Chris Dewhirst, Per Lindstrand, Don Cameron, Julian Nott, Angela Lewis and Charles Pierson.

Safe landings to you all.

RICHARD BRANSON & PER LINDSTRAND

FOREWORD

*I*N 1851 Gerard de Norval, in his preface to *Les Ballons — l'Histoire de la Locomotion Aêrienne*, wrote, 'It is with a special sort of courage, indeed, audacity, that we dare to document an aerostation for men. Our ignorance of the subject is particularly singular'.

Despite the rapid advances in education and media that have characterised our modern technological society, balloons still represent a mystery to most. Material technology has brought the balloon within the grasp of the 'average consumer', yet there is still little understanding of man's most majestic form of free flight.

This book is a step in the right direction, for, as we learn, our horizons are broadened, and as in ballooning there are no bounds. Many of the 'exotic sports' available pit the individual against the odds or nature. This is far removed from the group participation and highly social art of ballooning. The ascent of a balloon occurs only after the coordinated skills of a number of people have combined to ensure that the craft is assembled correctly, inflated, warmed and positioned for flight. The serenity of a silent departure from the launch field of the massive, colourful vessel is enjoyed not only by the ground crew but by all who are fortunate enough to witness the event.

We hope you enjoy the reading ahead of you. As you delve into the details of balloon flight, allow your imagination to fly free. Readers merely in search of excitement, be prepared to discover a totally new set of experiences. Although more than a century has passed since *Les Ballons* appeared, much ground has yet to be covered.

MAD, MAD BALLOONISTS

0600 HOURS.
The great burner roars in the stillness of dawn, forcing hot air into the inert, lozenge-shaped canopy on the ground. Slowly the envelope stirs, swells with air, rolls sluggishly across the wet grass until, like a giant phoenix, it rises ponderously from the dark field and stands erect, swaying gently in the early morning mist.

The dew evaporates from the soaking canopy and the balloon is wreathed in tendrils of steam and smoking water vapour. Its colours are dull and flat in the half light but, 80 feet above the ground, the crown of the envelope glistens brightly and reflects the first glow of dawn. In the traditional wicker basket the pilot completes his pre-flight checks: fuel pressures, burners, valve lines, vent lines, instruments and temperatures. The yellow and blue propane flame roars again, blasting more hot air into the envelope until the basket creaks and strains to leave the ground. The tether line is snapped open, the pilot orders 'Hands off!'

Serenely the balloon lifts into the sky. The world is suddenly calm, the Earth gently falls away, and the balloon is floating on the wind like a leaf.

Right now, in a dawn or afternoon field somewhere in the world, an aeronaut will be leaving the ground in a precarious-looking arrangement of wire, nylon and cane for a magical flight with the gods. Humans first ascended in these flying machines more than two hundred years ago and now, as then, dogs bark and chase the coloured canopies above, cattle stare stupidly at the flying humans, and children and adults look upwards and point in wonder. The miracle of flight is somehow demonstrated more graphically by these quiet, frail-looking craft than by any supersonic Concorde or

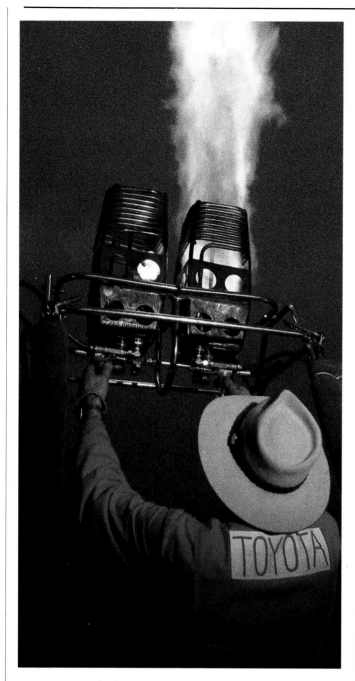

▲ *0605 hours* Sally Samins
▶ *0620 hours* Sally Samins

▶ Top inset: *Whatever the hour of the morning, there's always someone with a smile to wave you away . . .* Sally Samins
▶ Right inset: *. . . though the return reception may depend upon the landing.* Sally Samins

Previous page: *A full basket.* Sally Samins

ungainly Jumbo — and the joy of silent flight is being re-discovered by more people every year.

This renaissance in ballooning has certainly proven a boon to vintners of champagne around the world. After a person's maiden flight — many balloonists insist after *every* flight — a bottle or two is popped, joie de vivre flows into glasses and stomachs, and the experience becomes a mystical and hallowed memory. American Buddy Bombard has elevated this post-flight glass to almost an art form with his champagne de luxe ballooning. After dawn flights above the lyrical Italian countryside of Tuscany, Bombard spreads a white linen tablecloth, conjures up chilled tulip glasses, takes the best French champagne off ice, and a breakfast more in keeping with the court of Louis XVI complements the only way to begin a day whilst travelling through Europe. If you don't fancy the Italian countryside, Bombard provides the same de luxe service in France over

Burgundy and at Salzburg in Austria.

Because ballooning is now an international sport, or pastime, or hobby, it provides the balloonist with an ideal excuse to travel. And what better way to see another country than from the air, floating leisurely over valleys and streams and hills that would otherwise take a hard day's driving to see? For mountainous and desert regions it is sometimes the only way.

The only problem with ballooning in these remote areas is that the preparations can sometimes get out of hand. When a French pilot recently went to the Sahara Desert he ended up taking with him fifteen people, six tons of equipment, four lorries and two hot air balloons. The Sahara is the largest desert in the world, three and a half million square miles in area, so it was as well to go prepared. Pilot Dany Cleyet-Marrel, writer Alain Sèbe and film-maker Gerald Vien went south to Algeria in 1983 with a blue balloon named *Benamour* and a yellow balloon named *Benjamin*. They travelled across the Atlas Mountains and deep into the desert, into the Great Emptiness — the Kel Essouf.

▲ *The traditional post-flight celebration: back to Earth, but with bubbles still in the blood.* Sally Samins
▼ *De luxe flying with Bombard over noble châteaux and centuries-old estates.* Balloon Aloft

◄ *Riding the wind like silent chariots, hot air balloons fly over Leeds Castle in Kent.* Thunder & Colt Balloons

They drove to the dry stone villages of the M'zab with the flowing Arabic names of Béni Izguen and Ghardaia, where the strange, colourful balloons were celebrated with wonder and laughter by the villagers. 'It was difficult to say who was the most surprised by what they saw,' Cleyet-Marrel said, 'the Algerians or the balloonists.' To everyone everything was new, unexpected, and alive with differences. *Benamour* and *Benjamin* flew above the desert ergs, the great tracts of shifting sand such as the Great Occidental and the Cherch, vast marching dunes of barren solitude and emptiness.

And heat. With ambient temperatures as high as 45 degrees Celsius the temperature of the crowns of the envelopes reached 130 degrees at times in order to get enough lift — and this was in winter. This was a major problem with these desert flights. The envelope fabric 'cooks' and ages very quickly at these temperatures. Most of the flights were therefore made at dawn, during that precious hour or two when the desert is still cool

▲ *Ballooning with style in Europe — the best cheeses, fresh fruit, and French champagne.* Balloon Aloft

▶ *Drifting over the still, calm waters of a Tuscan lake — what better way to begin the day?* Thunder & Colt Balloons

16

◄ Benjamin *slowly climbs a massive dune in the Great Occidental Erg.* Dany Cleyet-Marrel

▲ *Inflating in the market place at Ghardaia draws a crowd as large as would a Mohammedan festival.* Dany Cleyet-Marrel

► *Not as easy as it looks! British Airborne Regiment recruits take that first, long plunge from an RAF gas blimp.* RAF Brize Norton

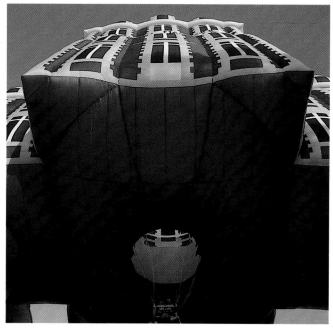

▲ *The* Château Balleroy *takes to the air in the grounds of the château itself.* Laurie Warner
▶ *Sheltering at an oasis.* Dany Cleyet-Marrel

from the bitterly cold nights. Landing presented retrieve problems, too. Flying speeds varied from between 10 and 25 knots, and dramatic swirls of wind would suddenly take the balloon into rocks and inaccessible areas with the four-wheel-drive lorries chasing after. Sewing machines were used frequently to repair tears and holes.

However, balloonists don't have to go to the ends of the Earth to enjoy themselves; Normandy will do. In June every year the late Malcolm Forbes used to invite celebrities, friends and balloonists, not necessarily in that order, to a balloon meet at the Château de Balleroy in Normandy. Balloonists were the honoured guests, and the weekend was a celebration of ballooning around the world.

On the lawns in front of the château Forbes would inflate some of his Special Shape balloons, including one of Balleroy itself. Special Shapes were one of his passions. He commissioned them from Cameron Balloons of Britain and took them on goodwill tours to friends and allies of the United States. One of the most stunning of these balloons was *Süleyman the Magnificent*, a 170-foot-high reincarnation of the sixteenth-century leader of the Ottoman Empire, a ruler already recorded by history as being larger than life; he personally garrotted both of his warrior sons. The modern *Süleyman* was taken on a goodwill tour to Turkey in 1988, where Forbes and his chief pilot, Dennis Fleck, managed three free flights out of seven inflations of this giant hot air balloon.

▲ Benamour *floats serenely through a rocky wadi*. Dany Cleyet-Marrel

◄ *Inhospitable, barren and forbidding; in the foothills of the Plateau du Tadermait*. Dany Cleyet-Marrel

▼ *One of the difficult retrieves from a Sahara depression*. Dany Cleyet-Marrel

If you're still looking for fun, try Ireland. There may not be a great amount of ballooning in the Emerald Isle, but what there is is certainly enjoyable. The Irish National Championships are held in September in the lakelands at Ballymahon in County Longford. Bally-mahon is found between the Royal Canal and the beautiful Lough Ree, but perhaps a more precise description of the championship location would be the Newcastle

House Hotel in Ballymahon. 'You might say that actual competition is secondary at this event,' says an American entrant, Robert Zirpolo. 'The most important detail for the organisers is to make sure there is a sufficient supply of "The Guinness" on hand.' The competitive tasks set at these nationals also differ slightly from the tasks set at, say, Albuquerque or Bristol.

One such task is the 'Flying Farmer'. Here the pilot takes off from the host inn and attempts to land at as many different farms as possible. At each touchdown he or she must convince the farmer or landowner, or both, that it is far more important for him to climb into the basket and come flying than it is for him to stay and work the fields. After several of these hops the land

below is populated by farmers and landowners all on their neighbours' farms; multiply this by the number of balloons flying and very soon the agriculture of the whole county has come to a virtual standstill. This economically disastrous situation is resolved by every-one meeting at a local pub. A point is awarded for each farmer carried aloft, and a bonus points system operates

▲ *From the sky above the Normandy countryside, the grounds of the Château Balleroy.* Jerry Young/Katz Eyes

for the lucky pilot able to persuade a member of the clergy to risk an ascent — two points for a priest, three for a bishop.

Another task unique to the Irish Nationals is where the pilot must fly the balloon onto one of the peat bogs that abound in this country. Without leaving the basket the pilot and crew must then gather as many frogs as possible, scoring a point for each live frog brought back to the bar at the inn. This task is not as easy as it might at first seem. But perhaps the most prestigious task of the championships is the race from the Newcastle House Hotel to the pub at Killashee, a flight to the north

▲ Süleyman the Magnificent, *1494–1566, reincarnated 1988.*
Cameron Balloons
▶ The Harley-Davidson, *one of Malcolm Forbes' collection of Special Shapes, under the somewhat dubious gaze of a gendarme. No doubt he is noting the absence of licence plates.* Alain Guillou (courtesy of Cameron Balloons)

▲ *Keeping a sharp lookout for priests and bishops over the land of the leprechaun in County Longford.* Robert Zirpolo

◄ *Approaching a peat bog in the 'frog' task: the bog is the brown area at centre left.* Robert Zirpolo

◄ **Left inset:** *Skimming over the River Shannon near Lanesboro.* Kevin Haugh

◄ **Right inset:** *An imposter in the land of the Guiness* Tom McCormack

of some twelve miles. For this task it is imperative that the publican at Killashee lay in extra supplies of 'The Guinness'. The winner is the first pilot to place an order at the bar. Zirpolo had a dream flight in the 1987 Championships when he landed barely a quarter of a mile from the pub door; his flight was so unexpectedly quick that the pub hadn't yet opened. 'We placed the basket on the bar and charged everyone five pounds to enter the pub,' this intrepid aeronaut recalls. This is the only task called for on that day of the championships, **the retrieve at Killashee being particularly arduous.**

Despite every honest intention, dawn flying is comparatively rare in Ireland. The 0600 calls are religiously adhered to, but the morning fog and mists often hang around until nine or ten o'clock, and only then can flying begin. The hospitality of the Irish is profound during these events and, what with the late morning launches, impromptu teas, scones and home-baked goodies in the many farmhouses, as well as 'The Guinness', most ballooning teams leave Ireland somewhat heavier on their feet than when they arrived. In recognition of the major cultural impact the sport has had on the country, the Galway Ballooning, Drinking and Musical Society was created. It is one of ballooning's rare honours to be admitted as a member.

On the other side of the Atlantic Ocean, in the state of New York, is an American version of the Irish meet. The Adirondack Balloon Festival also takes place in September, and there is no formal competition scheduled at all; the flying is purely for pleasure and goodwill. And the flying is excellent, above the beautiful countryside around Glens Falls in the north of the state. Cool nights and warm days produce easy flying conditions over the autumn hills, and in this gentle terrain the laid-back balloonist can fly until almost out of fuel and still land without problems.

▲ *In Monument Valley, Utah.* Laura Nelson (courtesy of Mary Woodhouse)

▶ *Balloonists in the United States have the choice of almost all possible landscapes. One of the rarer pleasures is flying through the Grand Canyon, following the Colorado River on its winding way to the Gulf of California.* Bob Barbarick

The Dutch hold a similar meet, the Balloonfiesta Brecklenkamp, invitation only from hosts Rien Jurg and Clemens Machielsen. The venue is in the grounds of a beautiful red brick manor house complete with its own moat, built in 1633, in which the balloonists stay. There are *no* planned morning flights at this very civilised assembly, the emphasis being on comradeship and fun and a party every night after the evening flight. Brecklenkamp ballooning is novel in that pilots and crews must carry their passports with them — only 500 yards to the north, east and west of the manor house lies the border with West Germany. This is international flying made easy.

South again to Africa where, even now, one can still see magnificent herds of wild animals in bush that has barely changed since humanity was still in accord with the natural world. In the Masai Mara of Kenya and the Serengeti of Tanzania over a million wildebeest and as many as 200,000 zebra migrate each year, charging spectacularly across the River Mara in their search for better grazing in the south. Moving with them, filtering through the dust of the great herds, roam the predators; the hyenas and jackals, the lions and cheetahs. There's no better way to view even a small part of this game than in one's own private aerial gallery, floating over the moving herds in an open wicker basket.

In 1962 the helium balloon *Jambo* did just that, being one of the first balloons to fly over eastern Africa. Pioneer British balloon and airship manufacturer Anthony Smith, with Alan Root and Douglas Botting, took off from the island of Zanzibar in the Indian Ocean to begin their balloon safari. They flew *Jambo* across Tanzania, the Masai Steppe and then the Rift Valley to the Serengeti Plain, filming the great herds passing beneath. These days this can be done with ease from the Governor's Camp and other lodges in the Mara Reserve, taking off at about 0630 to drift above the African bush alive with the scents of a new morning. The roar of the burner is the only sound to disturb the birds and animals, and amongst the howls, shrieks and clatter of the waking world below even that sound is usually lost in the general din. Touch down on the plains for a champagne breakfast while the beasts stare curiously at you for a change, and wait while the chase crew, often Masai, come in Land Rovers for the return drive through the bush back to camp. Shoot the animals at will, but only with a camera; the Serengeti and the Mara are wildlife sanctuaries. Ivory poaching unfortunately still takes place, the rare black rhinoceros have gone and the remaining elephant are decimated by the hunters' guns.

If your taste isn't for safaris and the Rift Valley, the cradle of Homo sapiens then perhaps the cradle of Christianity and Judaism can tempt you. Gideon Arbel

▲ *Gas (helium) balloons inflating for a promotion in the United Kingdom.* Steve Moss

is the pioneer of modern hot air ballooning in Israel, and that country's first international balloon meet was held as recently as 1988. Tel Arad was the venue, a town in the hot, dry deserts close to the western shores of the Dead Sea. Light, almost nonexistent winds make flying and landing easy above these ancient biblical lands, and by the third day of this fiesta a crowd of 50,000 had come to watch the balloons.

▲ *Near Tel Arad and the Dead Sea, the first Israeli international fiesta gets under way.* Brenda Speirs

◄ *An unconcerned giraffe continues its search for places to graze while a silent balloon passes above.* Thunder & Colt Balloons

▲ *Soaring above the golden Serengeti.* Jerry Young/Katz Eyes

◄ *Thousands drove by bus into the desert to watch the balloons fly.* Brenda Speirs

► *First cousins to the cheaper and more popular hot air balloons, gas balloons usually rely on traditional sand ballast and venting for control. A bag of ballast can be seen slung outside the basket.* Steve Moss

Above the dusty lands of the New Testament the balloons vie for airspace with the Israeli Air Force. Jet fighters swoop and roll above and at times below the balloons, their vapour trails describing perfect arcs in the blue sky. Below, the Dead Sea glitters dully, while the children in the Bedouin camps gaze upwards and point in wonder at the silent, colourful lighter-than-air craft, ignoring the noisy aeroplanes. The camels and goats ignore both with studied indifference.

This ballooning craziness seems to know no bounds, and has spread even to the inhospitable snows of the polar regions and the mountains. The first Arctic balloon meet was held in 1977 at Kiruna in Norbottens in the far north of Sweden, almost a hundred miles inside the Arctic Circle. Over bleak and dangerous Lapland hot air balloons took to the skies, flying gracefully above the snow-laden firs and concealed valleys below. Snowshoes, shovels and survival kits were issued to every flier; instructions on how to build an igloo were mandatory in every balloon.

Temperatures were down to –25 degrees Celsius, and after landing, survival became the first priority while the balloonists waited for the motor skidoos to make the retrieve; one night in the open would have been fatal. The low temperatures also affected fuel pressures, causing the propane gas to drop to as little as 25 pounds per square inch (psi) from the normal 80–100 psi. This pressure loss reduces the available power alarmingly, though one way to compensate is to heat the propane cylinders with an electric blanket before flying. It all makes ballooning in the Arctic a little different from the temperate green field variety.

◀ *A close shave.* Steve Moss
▶ *A cold and bleak launching site near Kiruna in Sweden, during the first ever Arctic meet in 1977.* Steve Moss
▼ *Like so many Chinese lanterns, hot air balloons tethered in the dark of evening.* Tim Blaisdell (courtesy Mary Woodhouse)

▲ *The joy of alpine flying. It's worth a sniffly nose for ballooning like this.* David Partridge, Air-2-Air
▶ *Lift-off in the sun and snow over traditional alpine chalets.* David Partridge, Air-2-Air

Mountain flying, too, brings its own peculiar dangers and thrills, not least being the retrieve. A dedicated and resourceful crew is a must for this type of ballooning. Above the mountains, the turbulent downward-swirling winds on the leeward side of a snowy peak are only equalled in their potential for disaster by the thrusting upward currents on the windward side, both threatening to slam a balloon into the mountain. Over the tops of the ranges can be found freezing fog, mist, mountain air waves and strange, unpredictable draughts of air that can carry the unwary pilot to disaster.

Kurt Ruenzi and Joseph Starkbaum of Austria were the pioneers of mountain flying in the 1970s, ballooning in the unknown winds above the Alps in summer and winter to find relatively safe peaks and accessible valleys over which to fly and land. Now regular meets are held at Zell Am See and the village of Filzmoos in Austria and, in Switzerland, at Mürren, venue for the High Alpine Ballooning Week, and at the Château d'Oex during winter, a true icicle meet. It is exhilarating, thrilling and sometimes dangerous work. Special survival kits of food and a tent are required equipment for Alpine ballooning, the cost being refunded afterwards if they are not used.

▲ *A fairy-tale above icing sugar mountains.* David Partridge,
Air-2-Air

Elsewhere around the world, at meets, fiestas, sports
events like the Olympic Games, celebrations and birth-
days, hot air and gas balloons are floating serenely over
fields and towns and cities. Right this minute someone,
somewhere is dragging themself out of bed in the small,
cold hours of the morning to taste the thrills and sublime pleasure of lighter-than-air flight. It can't only be
the promise of a glass of champagne.

▲ *High-altitude hang-gliding from balloons has become more popular with those for whom leaping off cliffs does not provide a sufficient buzz. The current altitude record stands at 36,700 feet by Briton Rory McCarthy. From such balloon launches hang-gliders have crossed the English Channel from above England to land in France.* Jerry Young/Katz Eyes

▶ *Wherever balloons fly they create great interest. The* **Pepsi** *balloon of Dick Wirth made the first recorded flight over the Great Pyramid of Cheops outside Cairo, and the desert scrub was alive with Egyptian spectators.* Jerry Young/Katz Eyes

▲ Top inset: *Yet wherever one flies, landing usually only serves to emphasise human mortality.* Jerry Young/Katz Eyes

THE BICENTENNIAL DECADE

*T*HE 1980s — the bicentennial decade of the first recorded flight by a human being — were to be an eventful ten years of international ballooning, with records made and broken in both gas and hot air balloons, airships once again appearing over the great cities of the world, Special Shape balloons spreading like mushrooms in weird and wonderful forms, and celebratory events held in the four corners of the Earth.

One of the strangest unofficial records of the 1980s was set in 1987, at the Bristol Fiesta in Britain. On the morning of 15 August, Henk Brink of the Netherlands took off in the 850,000-cubic-foot hot air balloon *Nashua*, with a double-storey basket beneath. On board this aerostat were an amazing fifty people, the greatest number ever to ascend in a balloon.

But first to France, where it all began.

THE BICENTENARY OF FLIGHT

1983 was the key year of the decade, and Paris the setting for the main event of the aeronautical calendar, celebrating that historic first flight of d'Arlandes and de Rozier in 1783. 'The riddle of eternal life has been solved,' a French commentator remarked at the time. In commemoration of that flight the Musée Aéronautique de France commis-

▲ *The record-breaking 850,000-cubic-foot* Nashua *hot air balloon, which carried fifty people aloft in a double-storey basket on 15 August 1987.* Cameron Balloons
◄ *The replica of the first Montgolfière flies above Paris in the summer of 1983, celebrating 200 years of manned flight.* Alain Guillou/Leica

sioned a replica of the original Montgolfière. Instead of the rag paper and linen envelope — what aviation authority would license that these days? — a more modern one of rip-stop nylon and Nomex (heat-proof nylon) was used, but coated so as to look like the original aerostat. Even the open all-round gallery was re-created.

The summer solstice of 1983 produced cloudless skies and warm, gentle breezes, perfect Parisian weather for the street cafés and restaurants. Elegant women and men thronged the boulevardes and avenues as a blue and gold Montgolfière once again flew above the roof-tops of Paris. Some of the sky-line would have been familiar to the first aeronauts, but the Tour Eiffel and l'Arc de Triomphe would have come as a shock. Not so much of a shock as the Concorde or the Space Shuttle, though.

Five days after this flight, nineteen gas balloons from around the world began to inflate in the Place de la

Previous page: Viking Maru *flies past the towers of Notre Dame in the Gordon Bennett Race.* J. Coutausse/Alain Guillou/Leica

Concorde in another salute. The Aero Club of France had organised a double event to commemorate the first manned gas balloon flight, by Professor Jacques Charles and Aine Robert, and also a Gordon Bennett Air Race. Entries in the latter were representative of their country, while those in the Charles and Robert race were private entrants. Both were distance races.

A crowd of almost a hundred thousand gathered in the centre of Paris but heavy rain, storm clouds and strong, gusting winds delayed the lift-off. 'It's the worst launch weather I've seen in thirty years,' stated one balloonist. A mid-afternoon squall threatened the whole event as Max Anderson and Don Ida of America took off in the translucent *Viking Maru*, followed by Cynthia Shields of America and Rien Jurg of the Netherlands in *Côte d'Or* and the combined Canadian/German team in *Augsberg*. Only a few minutes later Anderson spoke by radio to the control centre. 'We're being sucked up by this weather. I'd advise no further launchings until the conditions improve.' The flight director postponed the launch while a 35-knot squall swept across Paris, buffeting the tethered balloons and saturating their crews. *Viking Maru* found easterly winds while Shields and Jurg had a brush with disaster when *Côte d'Or* was slammed against the Tour Pleyel after a sudden down draught sucked the balloon down a hundred feet and into the forty-storey building. 'Oh boy, oh boy,' muttered Jurg. The weather was not ideal.

Meanwhile, after nearly an hour and a half's delay, the remaining sixteen balloons took off from a wet Place de la Concorde, flying low beneath a cloud base of only 1,500 feet. Last to launch was the Polish team flying *Polonez*. One pilot from the Netherlands — the Lowlands — was flying so low that his balloon only narrowly missed the Paris Opera House. He decided to give it away and landed shortly afterwards, and in a gesture of Gallic appreciation French officials presented him with a ticket for the entire winter season of opera. *Côte d'Or* and *Augsberg*, with a good half of the others, landed before nightfall in the Ile de France. *Polonez* soared away overnight and flew eastward towards central Europe, while *Viking Maru* found a wind with a touch of northerly in it and headed towards East Germany. Anderson and Ida were carried over Luxembourg that night and into West Germany and over the Rhine Valley the following morning. By the second afternoon they were approaching the East German border. They were not given permission to enter that country and so advised Frankfurt Air Traffic Control

that they would land near Bad Kissingen, a few miles inside the border. They had flown nearly 350 miles.

Anderson and Ida brought *Viking Maru* down near some woods, and on touchdown fired the explosive bolts to release the envelope from the basket. These wire cutters were experimental, not quite suitable for *Viking Maru*, and apparently left some wire strands intact — enough to carry the basket up again. At about 130 feet these strands finally parted under the strain and the basket plummeted back to the ground. A distant observer saw the balloon descend behind the trees and then saw the envelope rise again without the basket. It came to rest entangled in the branches of trees some three miles downwind to the east.

Max Anderson and Don Ida were found dead beside their basket. Reviewing the two hundred years of ballooning Anderson had earlier remarked: 'We understand it a little bit better now. I'm not sure that we fly it any better.'

The Polish team in *Polonez* won this commemorative race with a flight of 428 miles, landing near the Czecho-

▲ *One of the more daunting Special Shapes to be built in the 1980s. This giant dinosaur from Cameron's was for the 1988 Winter Olympics at Calgary in Canada.* Cameron Balloons
◄ *Ludwig van Beethoven returns to the Reichstag in Berlin during a Malcolm Forbes goodwill tour of the Federal Republic of Germany.* Cameron Balloons

slovakian border. But the celebrations were muted by the deaths of two such respected pilots.

France was also host to the World Hot Air Balloon Championships in 1983, at Nantes on the mouth of the River Loire. The visiting teams were billeted at the Château de la Pervenchère, north of Nantes in the Loire-Atlantique, a region of refreshing ocean breezes and splendid flying weather. Peter Vizzard of Australia won the championships of this celebratory year. On 21 November, before the magnificent Château de Versailles, a Montgolfière was inflated in the traditional manner, with its envelope supported between two poles over a pit of hot air. Exactly two hundred years after the first manned flight, a traditional Montgolfière rose again, in company with other hot air balloons and pilots from around the world.

But 1983 was not the only bicentennial to fall in this decade. In the southern hemisphere in 1988 a nation with a proud history of aeronautical pioneers was also celebrating.

▲ *Another commemorative Montgolfière of 1983 at a meeting in the Netherlands organised by trans-Atlantic pilot Henk Brink.* Balloon Aloft

Facing page: *Nineteen gas balloons inflate in the Place de la Concorde as a storm approaches.* Alain Guillou

▼ ▶ *Palace de Versailles, 21 November 1983.* Alain Guillou

THE GREAT
TRANS-AUSTRALIA
BALLOON CHALLENGE

Like ballooning, the nation of Australia is young, its history even shorter than that of aeronautics. Geologically the land is ancient, a remnant of the vast, lost continent of Gondwanaland, and its Aborigines have existed there for 40,000 years and more. The island continent came under no central direction until British settlement in 1788 and so, in 1988, Australians celebrated their two-hundredth birthday.

The epic voyage of the First Fleet that brought Europeans to Australia was re-enacted, culminating in a grand parade of sail of the world's tall ships in Sydney Harbour; aircraft buzzed over the valleys, the mountains and the deserts in a Round Australia Air Race; the last stockmen drove a great mob of cattle along the old stock routes by horse and whip; and hot air balloonists weighed in with a marathon — the Great Trans-Australia Bicentennial Balloon Challenge.

From around the world pilots and crews came with their traditional wicker baskets to join the birthday party, bringing cheer from seventeen countries of the European, American and Asian continents. The balloons had names as diverse as their owners: the *Dakota Roughriders*, the *Virgin Jumbo*, the *Sydney Opera House*, *Sun Kachina*, *Rosie O'Grady's Flying Circus*, *Takahiro* and even *British Bacon*.

The idea, naturally, came from a balloonist — former Australian hot air ballooning champion Ruth Wilson. Nothing on this scale across a whole continent had been attempted before. From Perth, on the Indian Ocean coast, the balloon teams would fly and drive their way 4,000 miles across Australia to Sydney, on the Pacific Ocean, incorporating eight competition flights from a schedule of ten in their journey — and all in sixteen days.

With a 20-knot-plus wind, the celebratory flight in Perth was cancelled, and the seventy-three teams packed their equipment and took the road north-eastwards, where the Challenge would begin.

From Perth it is a pleasant 160-mile drive to Merredin in the heart of the wheat-belt. But the weather systems across Australia move generally from west to east — in

Top inset: *Trans-Australia Challenge officials fly the helium meteorological balloon at Merredin to gauge wind speed, direction and heights. The answer: no flight.* Sally Samins
▶ *Over a dry saltpan in Western Australia.* Sally Samins
▶ Bottom inset: *The first lift-off in the Trans-Australia at Kalgoorlie: flying by the tailings of one of the gold mines.* Sally Samins

the same direction as the Challenge was travelling — and at sunrise the next morning the winds were still too strong for ballooning. The first competitive flight was also cancelled. It was 1 April.

The convoy of more than 600 people and 120 vehicles — Land Rovers, trailers, cars, campervans, buses, pantechnicon and gas tanker — set off on the 120-mile drive due east to Kalgoorlie, capital of the goldfields.

The morning of Easter Saturday was the next scheduled competition flight, with the standard dawn briefing and roll call at 0530 hours. A jet flight was also scheduled to take off from Kalgoorlie Airport at 0710, and the Department of Aviation imposed a late curfew on ballooning until the aeroplane left. 'Bugger it!' said Carolinda Moroney, pilot of the *Virgin Jumbo* Special Shape. At 0600 the conditions for ballooning were the best yet: an easterly wind of about 8 knots with a 1,000-foot cloud base. The wind increased, the desert sun brought on the thermals, and by 0800 it was gusting to 13 knots at the target zone on Cruikshank Oval. But the

pressure to fly was intense. It was the last scheduled flight in Western Australia and the shire had donated 15 ounces of gold as first prize. The task was declared on, a fly-in from a three to five mile radius.

There followed a dash along the dirt tracks of the old mines into the scrub. Within the hour the first balloons soared aloft over Kalgoorlie. Only forty balloons were launched, several pilots aborting take-off after being caught in ground thermals, and in the difficult conditions only four managed to drop their markers in the target zone.

Cruikshank Oval presented a contrast. Groups of European Australians enjoyed the spectacle, sitting at champagne breakfasts with glasses and silver goblets, while Aboriginal Australian families squatted on the ground sipping from tins of fizzy drink and talking in Nungara dialect. Above them the lighter-than-air craft battled wicked thermals. Australian George Day's *Coca Cola* balloon half collapsed in a wind shear until it was crescent-shaped. 'For one moment I thought we were

gone,' he said afterwards. 'It was very dodgy. And very frightening.'

A popular comment was 'I'm glad to be down,' but landing wasn't easy, either. Many balloons were blown towards the airport, and at one stage the runways were littered with deflated envelopes and overturned baskets. 'But, after all, it is an airport,' Canadian Alastair Russell, task winner, said with a grin.

The Challenge medical team of Dr Peter French and Sister Mary Anne Offner reported only minor bumps and bruises, but the balloons didn't fare so well, and throughout the day and into the night there was much stitching. In case of injuries in the more remote bush areas, the medical team were in contact with the Royal Flying Doctor Service by radio. The Challenge committee of Ruth Wilson, Geoff Tetlow and Phil Hanson, balloonists all, cancelled the evening task, though some balloons made 'free' flights with local residents. The lord mayor was one passenger, and that balloon landed, once again, at Kalgoorlie Airport.

The following morning some free spirits slipped in another flight, but the majority of the cavalcade set off early for the toughest drive of the Challenge: some 1,100 miles along the Eyre Highway to Kimba in South Australia with nothing in between except the occasional petrol garage, and two time zones to cross. The Australian Army, which supplied fifty soldiers to support the Hungarian and Polish pilots, motored in convoy, but the majority of the teams travelled separately across the flat emptiness of the red Nullarbor Plain, past dry salt pans and along the longest stretch of completely straight road in the world. Some said the drive was the toughest part of the Challenge. There were many punctures, a broken axle, clutch bearing, water pump, gearbox and differential, and one Land Cruiser actually lost a wheel while driving along. It doesn't only happen in the movies.

But in the middle of the Nullarbor, amidst the dry red earth and low scrub, came one of the highlights of the Challenge. Aussies actually run cattle on the less arid tracts of bush here, and on Madura Station the Toyota balloon team of Ross Spicer arranged a free flight.

The conditions at dawn were perfect: thin cloud at 3,000 feet, light southerly winds of 2 to 4 knots, and below, thousands of miles of scrub less than six feet high on which to land. Seven balloons lifted off in the chill morning air and drifted slowly above the perfect primal peace of the Nullarbor. From 1,500 feet one could see only more red plain in every direction except south, where a blue haze indicated the Southern Ocean. With the pilot lights as well as the burners turned off the silence was absolute, almost spiritual, like a cold empty church on a hot summer's day. The balloons completed their effortless flights with perfect landings, merely a gentle bump as the baskets touched down on the dry clay pans.

Then it was back on the road and eastwards into South Australia and the relative greenness of the Eyre Peninsula. Kimba is a town of only 1,400 people, and the sudden arrival of another 600 was a prodigious event in its history. 'It's the most exciting thing that's happened here since they brought in the water fifteen year ago,' a wheat farmer commented. The small town bulged with people in a cultural mayhem. There were American stetson hats, the trim red jumpsuits of the British Virgin team, the stylish khaki and blue battle-dress jackets of the Louis Vuitton crew, the jungle greens of the army, the convict canvas of Australians celebrating their exclusive heritage of 'selection by the finest judges in Britain' and even a 'lowlander' in clogs and black pantaloons.

◀ Tumbleweed *and* Goodspin *in an early morning 'free' flight above the Nullarbor Plain.* Sally Samins

▲ *The 130,000-cubic-foot* Sydney Opera House *takes off at last from Kimba.* Sally Samins
▼ *Mass launch from the Kimba Showground.* Sally Samins

▲ *Crews struggle to control their balloons as the wind rises, with gusts of over ten knots.* Sally Samins

Because of the two-day drive from Kalgoorlie to Kimba, no task was scheduled for the first morning, but thirty-five balloons made free flights from the showground launch site in ideal conditions. Many of the Kimba hosts were taken aloft for their first balloon flight, and Sweden's Ingemar Lilja, flying *Master Card*, contrived to land his host in his front garden. The wind increased during the hot day to a 10-knot south-easterly for the 'hare and hounds' task allocated for the afternoon. Sixty-nine balloons took off at 1530 hours on 5 April, including, for the first time, the massive *Sydney*

Opera House Special Shape. With 130,000 cubic feet of envelope, this Cameron balloon was the second largest Special Shape in the world and, because it has no crown vent, a 10-knot ground wind was the maximum in which pilot Chris Dewhirst was prepared to land. As it was, the *Opera House* dragged more than 100 yards across a fallow field before coming to rest. It's as well Australian paddocks tend to be on the large side.

At the 0530 briefing the following morning, the south-easterly winds were given as 10 knots on the ground by Wally Williams, the Challenge meteorology man and former Royal Australian Air Force pilot. There were good-natured murmurs of 'more like fifteen, Wally' from the assembled pilots. At 800 feet the wind was given as north-easterly, and the target nominated by the judges was 6½ miles to the west. The balloons took off from the Kimba Showground, but already there was wind shear, and Yorkshireman David Bowers had an interesting launch in *British Bacon*, swirling across most of the launch area before finally lifting away. *Opera House* wisely remained earthbound.

On completion of this task the half-way stage of the Challenge had been reached. Former gas and hot air world champion David Levin of America, flying solo in *Vitamin E*, was leading the points score with Jean-Robert Cornuel in the *Canson* balloon second. Joseph Stark-baum of Austria, runner-up in the 1987 world championship, was third, with a large group giving chase close behind.

Levin made the understatement of the event when he said: 'It was tricky landing in this wind.' Pilot estimates put the ground wind, which had increased dramatically since the launch, at 20 to 25 knots. Brenda Speirs, flying *Canadian Airlines* with an all-woman team, dragged more than 100 feet before her basket began to fill with earth and stop; her crew suffered bruises and one

▲ *Once aloft the flying was*
wonderful . . . Sally Samins
▶ *. . . but the landings were*
tricky. It's as well that
Australian paddocks are large.
Phil Castleton

▲ *One of the shorter landings.*
Sally Samins

◀ *Pilot Carolinda Moroney*
checks the billowing Virgin
balloon. Sally Samins

sprained ankle. Jean-Robert Cornuel landed heavily in *Canson* and fell across his co-pilot, Serge Brunias, who broke his ankle in three places. Brunias later had his leg set in plaster before flying home to France. Suzanne Milke of Denmark in the *J&B* balloon was thrown out in its heavy landing and the basket rolled over her, resulting in another broken ankle and an early flight home. Someone coined the phrase 'Carnage at Kimba'; Dr French and Sister Offner were busy that morning.

On the lighter side, Aden Wickes, flying in *Olympus*, landed right alongside Sabu Ichiyoshi in *TDK*. They raised the Australian and Japanese flags and toasted each other with champagne.

The balloonists bid farewell to Kimba and drove eastwards and then southwards into the verdant vineyards of the Barossa Valley. In the rolling hills of the Orlando Winery flying conditions were at last perfect. All but two balloons, which had equipment problems, took off for a hare and hounds task on a cloudless and windless 7 April. Alan Shaw, flying as hare in *Carrington Bubble*, played a devious game, with many height changes, and virtually stopped at one point so that some of the pursuing hounds overshot him. Levin was one of those caught out. Mark Wilson, the youngest pilot in the competition at twenty, dropped his marker from *Just Right* only 6 inches from the target centre to take first

▲ *In the green Barossa Valley flying weather was perfect.* Sally Samins

▶ Facing page: *'Shouldn't there be something else over the basket?'* intrepid aeronaut Peter Counsell asks. Sally Samins

▼ *Launching was at last straightforward — and straight up.* Sally Samins

prize. Ingemar Lilja came second, while Japan's Toru Takahashi, flying with his family, came third, to advance his overall position to second place. Levin still held onto overall first place by just 20 points. At this stage, any of the first ten scorers could still win the Challenge trophy.

Only one flight was scheduled for the vineyards, since a long drag could damage some very expensive vines, and that afternoon the moving village set off again. The next stop was Mildura in Victoria, a brandy and wine producing centre. There were reports of heavy flooding in Queensland and New South Wales, and Mildura, on the southern edge of this weather system, was cold, wet and windy.

The 0530 briefing at Mildura Airport was a disappointment. There was a period of calm between 0600 and 0700 suitable for flying, but the Challenge was now in fully controlled airspace and the Department of Civil Aviation would only permit launching between 0720 and 0800. By that time the wind had risen to more than 13 knots. At 0744 the black flag was hoisted at the control centre and the task was cancelled; ballooning is a sport of patience for both crew and spectator. The crowd of about 1,500 gathered around the airfield perimeter was obviously disappointed, but several balloons were inflated to show them what might have been.

The balloonists packed once again and headed north.

Broken Hill, the 'Silver City', a mining town in the outback of New South Wales, was a drive of just 200 miles through kangaroo and emu country, and at 1730 the first balloon flew over the city. Asbjorn Damhus of Denmark piloted the *Elgas* Special Shape in a clear quiet evening. In the half light at 0600 the next day Wally Williams gave a weather report of south-south-east winds of 8 to 10 knots on the ground, with a weak inversion at 700 feet. There was a murmur from the pilots, and Ross Spicer called out: 'You've told us what the weather's like inside, Wally, but what's it like outside?' There was a roar of laughter.

▲ *Landing in the outback.* Sally Samins
◄ *A mass launch of more than seventy balloons lifts off over the vineyards of South Australia.* Sally Samins

A double task was allotted: from a launch at the airport the first was a judge's declared goal with a flight minimum of 1,000 feet over the town, and then a hare and hounds somewhere out into the north-west.

Once more there were interesting landings, and minor bumps and grazes saw the medical team in action again. Drags of more than 50 yards were not uncommon. Ann Green of Britain, flying the largest balloon of the Challenge, *Yellow Pages*, recorded a 155 yard drag — she measured it. The general consensus amongst the pilots was that the wind was a little stronger than forecast. Joe

Kittinger said with a grin: 'It's the first time I've flown at 20 knots in an 8-knot wind!'

But the feature of this task was the distances flown. Ann Green landed 25 miles out of town, not normally a problem, but in bush country with no roads it was six hours before a four-wheel-drive lorry from the army reached her. Howard Solomon dropped his marker from an extraordinary height above the target and was last seen disappearing over the horizon to the north-west. A local said: 'This is Australia. There's nothing out there except the desert and Alice Springs — and that's 750 miles away.' Solomon's chase crew couldn't find him, so at 1300 the Challenge co-ordinator, Tim Molloy, took off in a light plane with Phil Hanson to search for him. Solomon had landed many miles out on Willarid-

gee Station, was all right, and was enjoying some tea and damper and Aussie hospitality.

Further flying that day was cancelled, and after five tasks Levin had increased his lead to 86 points. But Daryll Stuart had now moved into second place after a fine morning flight, 3 points ahead of Japan's Masahiko Fujito. The next morning's flight also had to be abandoned because of 15-knot winds, and after two cancellations the residents of Broken Hill were becoming a little

◄ *Bang on course for the hare marker.* Peter Counsell
▼ *Surrealist balloon.* Phil Castleton

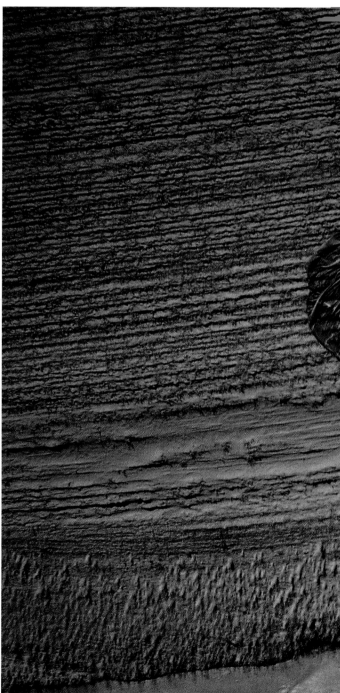

'restless'. A voluntary task was scheduled for the afternoon. The aeronauts were to attempt to fly-in and pluck a silver ingot off the top of an extended cherry picker in a school playing field, but the winds were still strong. Challenge director Ruth Wilson advised pilots not to fly unless they were skilled at high wind flying.

Fujito-san asked: 'How much is the silver ingot worth?' Eight thousand dollars was the reply. 'That's about one million yen,' he calculated. With his foot he traced a two foot square in the red earth. 'In Japan it would buy an area of ground that size, just large enough for one to stand in; not worth risking my life for.'

First to launch that windy afternoon was the Wyoming Wild Bunch with Jerry Elkins in *Tumbleweed*, but at 400 feet above the town the wind took the balloon to the west of the cherry picker. Elkins passed two streets away and landed in a gully with an easy 10-yard drag. Alastair Russell was the next to launch in *Spirit of Canada* but he, too, chose the wrong height and line. He eventually passed well to the west. Sunset was at 1749 and the launch period closed at 1730, but at 1727 another balloon rose into view above the rooftops.

It was *Tumbleweed* again. Somehow the Wild Bunch had retrieved, driven back to the launch area, and with the help of the Challenge officials inflated again for a

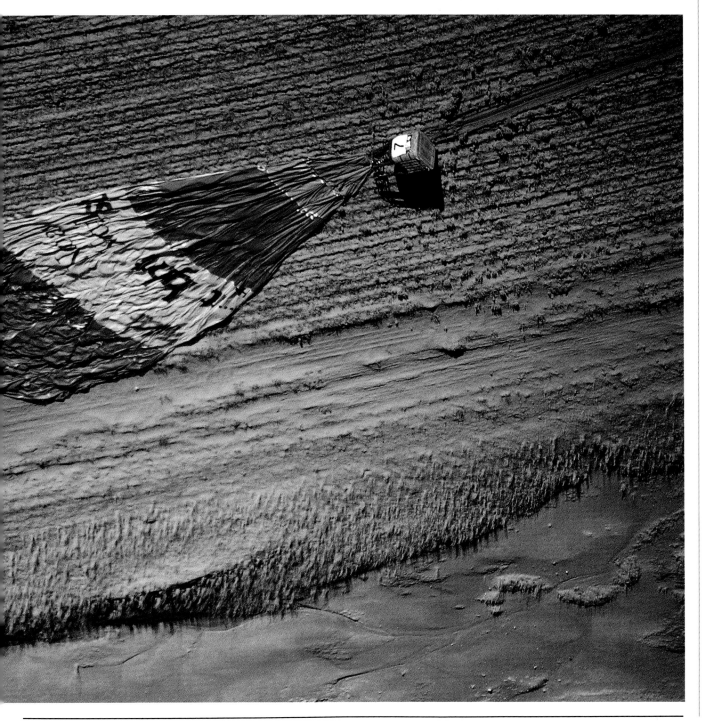

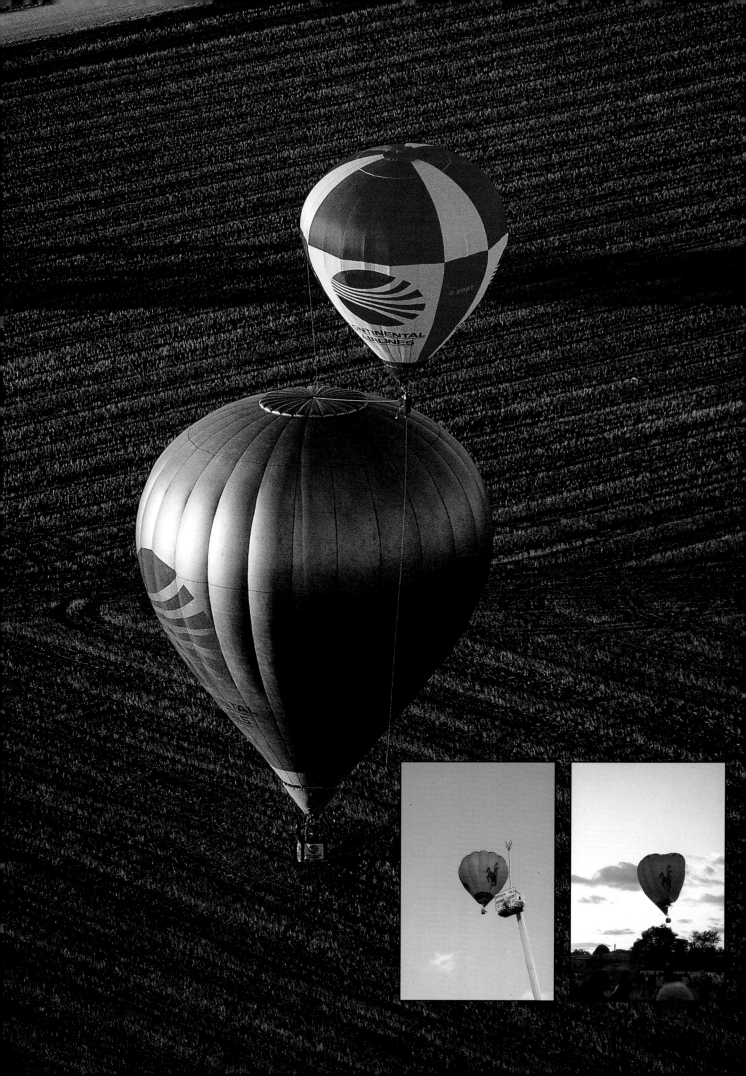

second attempt at the ingot. They kept low this time, hedge-hopping over the town on a good line and keeping north of the field. The yellow and brown *Tumbleweed* rose to 300 feet as Yentser manoeuvred to the south a little, and then he vented to come down over the target. Hot air spilled out of the crown of the balloon, drawing colder air in through the throat, and *Tumbleweed* dropped rapidly towards the cherry picker just 60 feet above the ground.

The wicker basket passed the silver ingot at the same height but 30 feet to the north and still descending. A field of upturned faces cheered as the burners roared, but the balloon kept dropping out of the sky. Yentser said afterwards: 'I thought we might get lift in time so I kept burning, but I'd left it too late.' *Tumbleweed* swooped over the field towards the houses alongside and swept through a tree top towards the back of number 113. A woman startled by the roar of the burners peered out of the window next door in some alarm. Elkins shrugged his shoulders and waved to her.

The next instant the basket slammed into the eave of the house, throwing the three men violently forward and almost out, and then tilted through 45 degrees. The burner flames roared into the balloon fabric, sending yellow fire licking up the side of the envelope. Silhouetted against the fading sunlight, the envelope dragged the basket, with the men grimly hanging on, up the sloping tin roof to its apex and down the other side. *Tumbleweed* at last started to rise again, just clearing the power lines along the side of the road with the basket swinging like a pendulum beneath the envelope. At 250 feet the crew regained control and brought the balloon down to a gentle landing close to the gully where they'd landed before. The medical team got there almost before the balloon.

Bruised, cut and shaken, the Wild Bunch survived the crash. The damage to number 113 could be repaired: *Tumbleweed* had a 6-foot-square hole burnt above the throat. The sympathetic townsfolk of Broken Hill presented them with a gift of 1,000 dollars in appreciation of their effort; balloon insurance paid for the 2,000-dollar damage to the roof. And then it was back on the road again, and just under 500 miles to Dubbo in the east.

The heavy rains had passed and the country was becoming more green and lush the further east the Challenge travelled. Dubbo is on the Macquarie River, and the launch site was alongside the river in a green meadow. Thirty-five balloons made free flights on the morning of the twelfth, but the first scheduled task that afternoon had to be cancelled because of thermal activity. The atmosphere in the evening was full of excitement during the town fair, and two balloons were tethered in the main street, where Britain's Kim Hull played games for the crowd in a cloud hopper.

On the fifteenth day of the Challenge the weary pilots and crews gathered by the river for the last 0530 briefing from the equally weary officials. Flying conditions were good, with a light and variable easterly blowing, no traffic expected at the airport, and airspace available to 5,000 feet. Wally Williams' weather report at last had the approval of the pilots amidst some good-natured bantering. A double task was designated — a hesitation waltz. This was the last competition task but points tallies were so close that a mistake by any of the leaders would let others through. The balloons to watch for were the deep red *Vitamin E* of Levin, the dark blue and black canopy of Stuart, and the yellow and orange envelope of Fujito-san. Chasing them hard was Britain's Chris Kirby flying *Continental Airlines* — a good flight here could put him amongst the first three.

At 0615 the balloons began to rise above the oval, over the river towards the first target. Brenda Speirs' team in *Canadian Airlines* had finally relented, and for the first time in the competition carried a man. She was chasing Australia's Rosalind Davies in *PAL*, presently lying ninth overall, for the highest women's position.

▲ *The burners roar in the dawn for the last time.* Sally Samins
◀ Facing page: *During a take-off from Dubbo the* Continental *cloud-hopper flies with its big brother.* Sally Samins
◀ Facing page insets: Tumbleweed *descending towards the cherry picker during the silver ingot fly-in and crashing into the roof of 113 O'Neill Street at Broken Hill.* Phil Castleton

▶ Inset: *At the prize-giving dinner at Circular Quay in Sydney, (left to right) Captain Daryl Stuart (second place), Ruth Wilson (director), David Levin (first place), and Masahiko Fujita (third).* Sally Samins

▼ *Graeme Scaife of Sussex (right) and his crew, with their tribute to the Challenge weather man, Wally.* Sally Samins

The closest marker to the first target was less than a foot from the centre, and the first rumours said it was Stuart's ribbon. *Vitamin E* drifted high and to the right between the two targets, but Levin corrected to throw a good marker at the second. But early rumours said that Stuart had beaten him once again. It would be poetic for an Australian team to win the Australian Bicentennial Challenge: both Stuart and Levin agreed that there would be only a few points difference whoever won.

▲ *Hedge-hopping taken to the nth degree.* Sally Samins
▶ *The* Virgin Jumbo *over Australia.* Phil Castleton

◄ *Above a bend of the Macquarie River at Dubbo.* Phil Castleton
▲ *Upon closer reflection.* Sally Samins

They now had to wait for the results to be computed.

This last task had its lighter moments, too. David Bowers' *British Bacon* — christened the Pommie Pig by the Aussies — was officially retired at Dubbo after eleven years of flying. Bowers was flying alongside the Aboriginal flag balloon of Australian Joe Blitz; he waved and called out: 'Hello, Joe, how are you?' 'Fine,' replied Blitz. 'By the way, your balloon's on fire.' As he spoke a piece of burning fabric drifted past Bowers and into his basket. He grabbed the fire extinguisher and sprayed the burning scoop and canopy. 'I thought it was time to retire her,' he said.

Just before midday the champagne was taken off the ice, glasses distributed, and the results posted. Levin had held onto first place by only 13 points from Stuart, with third place going to Fujito, a further 18 points behind. 'It was too close for comfort,' said a relieved Levin, 'but what a way to end the Challenge!' Kirby's late charge left him fourth, while Ros Davies maintained her ninth position to finish as the highest woman challenger.

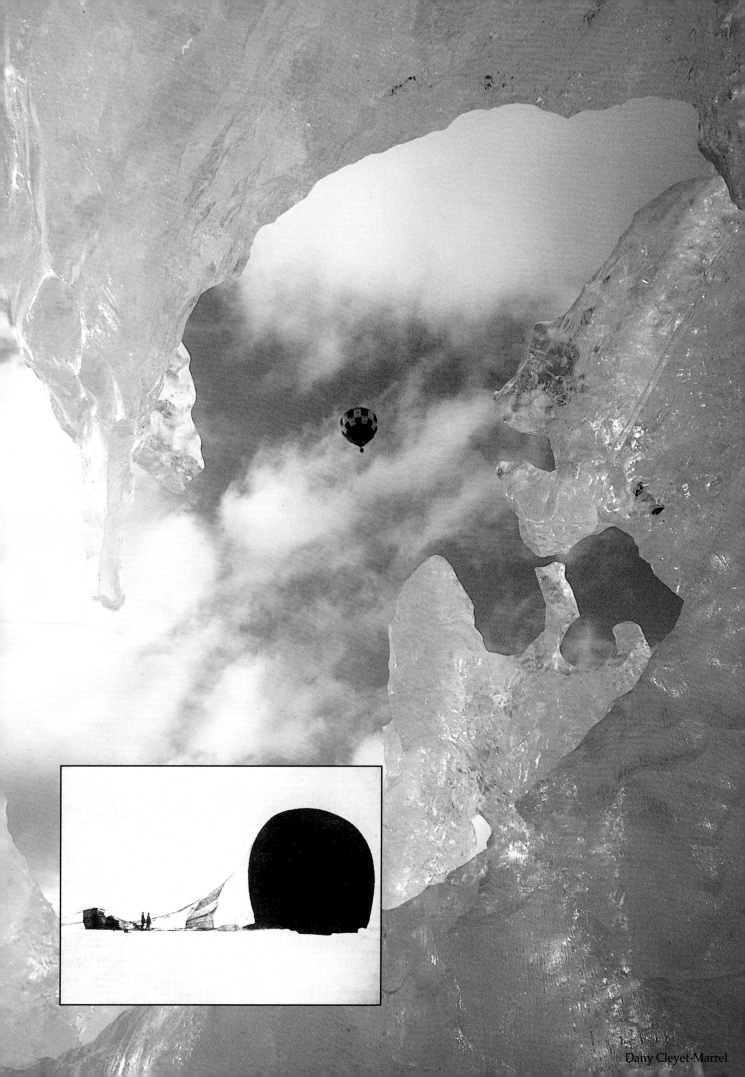

Dany Cleyet-Marrel

WITHIN THE ARCTIC CIRCLE

From the hot, parched deserts of Australia to the cold, ice deserts within the Arctic Circle — and Spitsbergen. Belonging to Norway, the barren, isolated island of Spitsbergen is one of the Svalbard group, situated across latitude 80 degrees north. Only 600 miles from the North Pole, this bitterly cold land supports the most northern community in the world, Ny Aalesund, and has been witness to a remarkable succession of flying tragedies almost in the heroic mode of the Greeks.

It was in 1897, from Danish Island just off Spitsbergen, that Salomon Andrée of Sweden left for the North Pole in the ill-fated hydrogen balloon *Eagle*. However, he had not known of the severe effect the sub-zero temperatures would have on hydrogen gas, and after an almost disastrous lift-off in freak winds he found that the lifting capacity of the gas was drastically reduced. Despite his jettisoning all the ballast, the basket kept hitting the pack ice below; after sixty-five hours the hydrogen had no further lift and *Eagle* settled onto the tumbled pack ice for the last time. Andrée and his two companions, Nils Strindberg and Knut Fränkel, set off to walk back to Europe across the ice. They reached uninhabited White Island, some miles northeast of Spitsbergen, and there died a painful and lonely death of trichinosis.

▲ *Inflating on the sea ice north of Spitsbergen, with the ice-strengthened support vessel standing by.* Dany Cleyet-Marrel

◄ Facing Page: *Through the ice, lightly. Dany Cleyet-Marrel.* Inset: *Salomon Andrée's* Eagle *hydrogen balloon during inflation at Spitsbergen, July 1897; the first aerial attempt on the North Pole.* Royal Aeronautical Society

▼ *Flying over the end of a glacier towards Spitsbergen.* J. Becker (courtesy Dany Cleyet-Marrel)

The North Pole was attempted again from Spitsbergen in 1907 and 1909 by American Walter Wellman. He used a French-built airship, but both flights ended by ditching in the Arctic Ocean and Wellman and his team were picked up by ship. The next expedition to the Pole set off from Ny Aalesund; polar explorer Roald Amundsen of Norway and pilot Umberto Nobile of Italy took off in 1926 in the airship *Norge*. They succeeded, dropped flags onto the ice below at 90 degrees north, and continued westwards to Alaska as the weather deteriorated. Ice actually formed on the propellers of the engines, and damaged the hull fabric when it was eventually thrown off by centrifugal force. The radio broke down and the sun compass couldn't be used because it had iced over, but Nobile landed the *Norge* safely at Nome after a flight of seventy-two hours and 3,400 miles. The two men had unfortunately quarrelled during the flight and parted as enemies.

Two years later Nobile took to the air again from Ny Aalesund, now leading his own expedition to the North Pole in the airship *Italia*. It was a disaster. *Italia* reached 90 degrees north after mapping islands off the Russian and Canadian Arctic coasts, but on the return journey flew into severe storms and ice collected alarmingly on the hull. Eventually unable to support the weight of these massive sheets of ice, *Italia* crashed onto the pack ice below, crushing the control car and one of the engine nacelles. Men, equipment and supplies spilled out onto the ice and the airship, now lighter, rose back into the air with six men trapped in the undamaged engine nacelle. The *Italia* was never seen again. During the many international rescue attempts three aeroplanes were lost, eight flight crew — including Roald Amundsen in a sea-plane — were killed, and eight men of the original expedition died. There were eight survivors, including Nobile.

It wasn't until 1985 that lighter-than-air craft returned to the islands. French polar explorer Jean Becker and pilots Bruno Dupuis and Dany Cleyet-Marrel took two hot air balloons, an ice-strengthened sealing vessel, and two tons of propane for forty-five days of flying and filming around Spitsbergen. The project included a flight over the Spitsberg itself (5,617 feet) and a seven-hour flight over the glacier ice fields to the capital, Longyearbyen. They filmed polar bears, reindeer, walruses and, from a trapeze slung from the envelope, the balloons themselves. One of the dangers they found was the strong winds that would whip across the ice without warning. It was just such a wind that had caught Andrée when he took off.

The last part of the expedition took the sealing vessel northwards into the frozen sea until her way was blocked by tumbled ice. In the biting cold the two balloons were discharged, inflated on the snow and then launched. For five hours the balloons slowly drifted over the silent white sea, above the ice flowers, the ice rind and the nilas of the freezing Arctic Ocean. Those not in the balloons followed beneath in the sealing vessel and inflatable dinghies. The only mishap the expedition suffered was a confrontation between three hefty one-ton walruses and one of the inflatables. The dinghy beat a hasty retreat from the walruses' two-foot-long tusks.

LE RADEAU DES CIMES

It's fitting that in this bicentennial decade one of the more unusual events should have been scientific, for from the early years of ballooning ascents were made for scientific studies. The first such flight was from Paris on 24 August 1804, by the respected physicists Joseph Guy-Lussac and Jean Baptiste Biot. They had been commissioned by the Science Academy of France to check the amazing reports made by another balloonist, Étienne Gaspard Robertson, following an ascent the year before. Amongst 'Professor' Robertson's claims was one that, at high altitudes, the atmosphere was replaced by 'fumes' and the strength of the Earth's magnetic field was reduced. Guy-Lussac and Biot were able to reassure the concerned Academy that all was as it should be aloft.

Since then, balloons have been used to aid scientific research in a variety of ways, but one of the more unusual adaptations occurred in 1986 when a scientific expedition set off for South America. This French-conceived project had the support of UNESCO, ORSTOM

▲ Le Radeau des Cimes *above the equatorial forest of Montsinery in French Guiana.* Dany Cleyet-Marrel
▶ *A worm's eye view of the strange 'ship of the forest'.* Dany Cleyet-Marrel

(Office de la Recherche Scientifique Outre-Mer), CNRS (Centrale Nationale de Recherche Scientifique) and the French Ministry of the Environment. The objective was to study the ecology of the equatorial forest canopy of French Guiana, the tree tops some 160 feet above the forest floor — *les cimes*. This had never before been possible, and on 25 September a team of botanists, entomologists, tropicalists, photographers and balloonists descended quite literally onto the Forest of Mont-sinery, one of the last unexplored equatorial regions. This descent was controlled by Dany Cleyet-Marrel, in a 106,000-cubic-foot hot air balloon, and led by Francis Hallé, Professor of Botany at the Montpellier University.

Suspended from this Montgolfière instead of a basket was a circular wooden platform on which were the burners and fuel tanks, and around this platform was a massive air-inflated rubber raft 23 feet in diameter — *le radeau*. Between the rubber tubes of the raft was slung a nylon netting, and the area of the radeau measured some 2,700 square feet. Base camp for the expedition was set up at Couleuvre Crique, 43½ miles from Kouron, the capital town of the region. The complete team numbered twenty when Geneviève Michon and Hubert de Foresta, equatorial forest experts, joined from the Congo.

Le radeau des cimes moved like an ancient sailing vessel, slow and cumbersome, almost sluggish in the light tropical airs. It drifted across the forest canopy exploring the little-known world of the insects, animals and flora that never leave the tree tops, that never touch the ground. The balloon would be anchored to the branches by ropes and the scientists would collect samples and

specimens from the edges of the raft as it rested on the foliage. They used pollen traps and insect traps, and took clippings of the blooms and leaves that live in this strange, self-sufficient and largely unknown eco-system suspended high above the tangled undergrowth.

Landing the unwieldy balloon was difficult, and the first attempt was unsuccessful. Selecting a desirable group of tree tops had to be done well in advance so that the raft could be manoeuvred into position in time. Cleyet-Marrel also used a cloud-hopper (sky chariot) to leave the raft and collect specimens from farther afield.

At night the balloon was deflated, the envelope laid out over the platform extension, and the raft would rest on the tree canopy, anchored by its ropes. The nocturnal life of the forest then filled the expedition's world with sound, a cacophony of strange insect and animal

▲ *Deflated and resting on the tree-tops.* Dany Cleyet-Marrel
▲ Inset: *The retrieve begins as* le radeau *alights on the River Compte after a month in the forest.* Dany Cleyet-Marrel

noises, of unexplained crackles and rustles and sudden crescendos of noise. Ultra-violet lamps were used in the deep equatorial darkness to attract the unseen night insects to the airborne laboratory.

The expedition lived for a month in the fecund world of the tree tops before *le radeau des cimes* finally descended, to float like a giant insect itself upon the muddy waters of the River Compte on 29 October. A month living in the forest canopy isn't long, yet the expedition gathered valuable ecological information and proved that this was an easy and relatively cheap way to study this environment.

ALBUQUERQUE

Throughout this bicentennial decade the various national events, championships and world championships continued with generally increasing numbers of people and balloons. In 1989 two major milestones in balloon manufacturing occurred. In the United Kingdom Cameron Balloons of Bristol recorded the manufacture of its two-thousandth balloon, while in the United States the Balloon Works of North Carolina recorded its three-thousandth balloon. Add to these figures the increasing productions of Thunder & Colt and Raven, plus Semco, Avian, Adams, Eagle, Galaxy, Piccard and Kavanagh, and some idea of the the world-wide expansion of ballooning can be found.

Zany balloonists meet and talk and drink and occasionally fly at gatherings around the world, but the greatest gathering of them all occurs in New Mexico. Here, in the autumn weather of October, they arrive by road, rail and air in the southern ranges of the Rocky Mountains and Albuquerque, set on the Rio Grande. The first balloon meet here was organised by Bill and Sid Cutter in 1972, when about 30,000 spectators watched fourteen balloons take to the sky above the traditional lands of the Pueblo Indian. The following year the Albuquerque meet was billed as the first World Hot Air Balloon Championships, and sixty balloons attended. This inaugural event was won by Dennis Flodden of America, using what was considered at the time to be an unsuitable lightweight basket. Bill Cutter took second place, with Janne Balkedal of Sweden third.

Now the Albuquerque International Balloon Fiesta is host to 500 balloons for the annual October bash, surely the largest gathering of balloons in the world. The Bristol meet in Britain was host to 200 balloons in 1988, the second largest fiesta. It was in Albuquerque that Coy Foster first flew a cloud hopper, the one-man balloon developed by Brian and Kathy Boland in the late 1970s. This flight led to Foster's fascination with this smallest of aerostats, and he now holds most of the FAI (Féderation Aéronautique Internationale) records for this class.

The various tasks for hot air balloon competitions were standardised by Nigel Tasker and Martin Moroney during the British Championships of 1976 and first used in the World Championships at Castle Howard near York in 1977. Because of the unique weather conditions

▶ Over page: *Mass ascent at the Albuquerque Fiesta, the largest balloon meet in the world.* Dr Michael Wall (courtesy Mary Woodhouse)

◀ Facing page: *Too many to count.* Dr Michael Wall (courtesy Mary Woodhouse)

▶ *Beware the power lines and cacti when landing.* Tim Blaisdell (courtesy Mary Woodhouse)

▼ Bottom: *At the Rio Grande, south of Albuquerque.* Balloon Aloft

▲ *How the beautiful Steier Mark appears to a balloonist, and how it appears on his map.* Balloon Aloft

◀ *Whichever way one looks at it, riding in a cloudhopper is seat-of-the-pants flying.* David Partridge/Air 2 Air

▼ *One's own personal chariot of fire, though this balloonist lacks the confidence and faith expected of a pilot.* Jerry Young/Katz Eyes

of Albuquerque — a mile above sea level — variations of the rules have produced some strange tasks. One of these is the Albuquerque Blackjack, an aerial version of vingt-et-un. Pilots have to land their balloons on squares on the ground marked with the values of play-

ing cards: a pilot can hold, go for pontoon and go bust.

This calls for great flying skill which is helped by the 'Albuquerque Box'. There is a variation of wind direction at different altitudes which will turn a balloon through 90 degrees, and the beauty of it is that the

necessary change in height can be as little as 50 feet. It's possible to fly for hours over Albuquerque and land only feet away from the launching point. It's a dream for retrieving, but one should keep an eye out for the cacti and thorn bushes.

▲ *The beginning of the 1987 World Championships at Schielleiten, near Gräz in eastern Austria. Balloon Aloft*

FORBIDDEN FLIGHTS IN OLD CATHAY

The 1980s saw a remarkable change in the political climate of the world, a gradual thaw between the major ideologies, and one of the benefits of this came to international ballooning. The vast, mysterious almost forbidden land of China was slowly opened to foreign travellers. Even Chinese-controlled Tibet is now partly accessible.

A modern hot air balloon had been taken to China in the 1970s. Malcolm Forbes took a balloon on a goodwill tour after the United States' belated recognition of the People's Republic. However, he was only given permission for tethered flights. 'We wanted to leave them the balloon when we went home,' Forbes said, 'but we weren't going to if we couldn't show them what they were for. Balloons are for flying.' During the last morning the crew slipped the tether line and the balloon was up and away, to the alarm and annoyance of the Chinese authorities. This alarm turned into some consternation and suspicion when the balloon and Forbes landed in a military base. The whole crew was detained for several hours for questioning. All was forgiven that evening at a banquet held in the visitors' honour. 'A balloon is a happy thing,' said Forbes.

▲ *A young Chinese woman meets her first balloon.* Jerry Young/ Katz Eyes

Then, in September 1985, Australians Judy Lynne and Peter Vizzard were invited to China and asked to bring two hot air balloons with them. They were to fly the balloons as a platform to take aerial photographs for the commemorative book *China: The Long March*, celebrating the fiftieth anniversary of the beginning of Mao Tse Tung's campaign. The flying was confined to the area around Ruijin and Yudu in Jiangxi province, in the south of the country. Some nine ascents were made.

Two years later, immediately after the World Championships in Austria, the Hong Kong Balloon and Airship Club was invited into China for more photographic work, for the pictorial book *Over China*. This time it was in the beautiful green and misty Guilin region of Guangxi Zhuang Zizhique province, 250 miles northwest of Guangzhou. In mid-September 1987, four hot air balloons, 6,000 litres of propane gas and two cases of French champagne were driven from Hong Kong to Guilin in two Chinese Army lorries for this ten-day expedition. Two of the Hong Kong balloons, bearing such blatant capitalist names as *Cathay Pacific* and *DHL*, flew over Guilin itself. They took off from Seven Star Park in the first light of dawn, startling the Chinese at their early morning exercises. Soldiers in the olive green of the People's Liberation Army worked alongside Hong Kong club members in white overalls to inflate the balloons, while the Guilin citizens watched in some amazement, their 'shadow boxing' routines forgotten.

The stalwarts of this interesting Hong Kong flying fraternity — Mike and Dawn Bradley, Doug Gage, Ron Pattison, Adam Takach, Garry Ogg and Paul Gianniotis

◄ *Floating through classical and inspiring Guilin.* Jerry Young/ Katz Eyes
◄ Facing page: *Above Guangxi Zhuang Zizhiqu province, China, 1987.* Jerry Young/Katz Eyes

— then took the balloons south for flying and photographing over and around Langshou on the River Li. The colourful aerostats drifted silently between grey-blue limestone peaks that rise straight from the green plains of this karst country, and floated past deserted caves above the intensively farmed river valley below. This strange landscape of pointed hills has been the inspiration for centuries of classic Chinese watercolours, for the painting of delicate china itself, and for the sublime, lyrical poetry of the Tang dynasty and others. While the un-lettered Charlemagne (734–814) was rampaging through western Europe, the poet Han Yu (768–824) was writing of Guilin:

> *The river is a blue silk ribbon,*
> *and the hills, like blue jade hairpins.*

Other flights were made from the villages of Bashai, Xing Ping and Jili along the River Li, but landing was always difficult, with drops onto river banks and pathways between paddy fields, and retrieves by river boat on the shallow, quickly flowing Li. Crowds of curious Chinese people materialised wherever the balloons launched or landed, eager to help but playing havoc with the crops. Many of the flights were filmed by Central China Television, and the resulting documentary was later broadcast to an audience of 200 million. Twelve free flights and six tethered flights were made during this last foray into China.

◄ Facing page: *In a rose-fingered dawn,* DHL *drifts slowly over a hazy River Li.* Jerry Young/Katz Eyes
▼ *In a nation with a population of more than a thousand million, farming is intensive — and landing difficult.* Jerry Young/Katz Eyes

▲ *Capitalist advertising stands brazen and harsh against a sunrise in the Middle Kingdom.* Jerry Young/Katz Eyes

◄ *Dawn in the outback before the disaster.* Steve Strike, Outback Photographics

DESERT DISASTER

The 1980s were also witness to the worst hot air ballooning disaster yet recorded. On Sunday, 13 August 1989, four balloons took off at dawn from the Santa Teresa Mission road, ten miles south-east of Alice Springs in central Australia. They were taking holiday-makers for a sunrise flight in clear, calm conditions. One of the balloons was the large black and orange VH-NMS, of 260,000 cubic feet, carrying twelve passengers and pilot Anthony Fraser in the large wicker and cane basket. After ten minutes' flying all the balloons had reached 3,000 feet and were close enough to take photographs of each other.

In one of the balloons was passenger Dr Irene Fielder from Germany. 'I could see one of the balloons rising quite fast under another one,' she said. 'The lower balloon [VH-NMS] then came up and hit the other balloon. Its top was touching the basket and it was shaking the passengers around. Then the lower balloon ripped and started to move away.'

In the upper balloon was passenger Geoff Smithers, who later said: 'We didn't see it coming — suddenly it was there. There was ripping as the top of the balloon below us tore apart, then you could hear a great rush of air. Its top was torn to shreds. Some people on our balloon screamed, but there was no sound from down below.'

Pilot Anthony Fraser turned on all burners to try and keep the envelope in shape as VH-NMS quickly lost height, five gores torn apart. The pilot of the upper balloon sent a Mayday radio call to Alice Springs air traffic control. The black and orange balloon continued to lose height until it was about 600 feet above the bush, when the envelope completely collapsed.

Ken Watts, pilot of the fourth balloon, was watching. 'I couldn't believe what I was seeing,' he said. 'The balloon just completely deflated and plummeted straight down to the Earth. It was a sickening sight.'

A cloud of dust marked the spot where it hit the ground. All thirteen people on board died, their bodies huddled together and their arms wrapped around each other in a last gesture of comfort.

◄ *The ill-fated* VH-NMS *hot air balloon taking off in the outback near Alice Springs.* Steve Strike, Outback Photographics

ON THE WIND AND A PRAYER

THE HISTORY OF BALLOONING

FROM THE dawn of time people have aspired to fly. In every culture their gods have come from the sky, endowed with the magical power of flight; sometimes with heavy-duty wings on their shoulders, sometimes with sportier models on their heels, and sometimes ascending by the Rolls Royce of flight — a golden halo about their heads.

From the cradle of western civilisation came the ingenious Greek explanation that the Sun was carried across the sky on the back of a winged chariot pulled, of course, by winged horses. Another Greek myth recounts the first air disaster. When Daedalus and Icarus escaped imprisonment from the labyrinth on Crete by flying from the island, young Icarus plunged from the sky into the wine-dark sea and drowned. He had flown too close to the Sun and his feather and waxen wings had melted.

In the first century BC the Nazca Indians of Peru may already have flown in some type of hot air balloon. This supposition is based upon designs on a pottery artefact in Lima, and upon the puzzling lines and piles of stones stretching across 200 square miles of the Plain of Nazca. The stones are meaningless — until seen from the air, when they form patterns of massive birds and directional markings. A primitive hot air balloon, copying the pottery design and using only materials available to this pre-Inca

The renaissance introduced a more scholarly attitude to flying. The amazing Leonardo da Vinci took up Bacon's theories and experimented further with hollow wax models in water. His keen interest in flight resulted in a 35,000 word study but, ahead of his time like Bacon, his work was not published until the late eighteen hundreds.

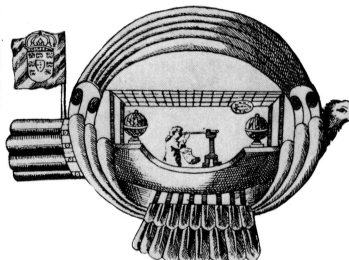

▲ *An artist's impression of the first air crash: Daedalus watches as his son, Icarus, falls from the sky into the Mediterrenean Sea.* Royal Aeronautical Society
▶ *De Gusmão's* Passarola — *innovative, but never likely to leave the ground.* Royal Aeronautical Society

civilisation, was built and flown successfully in Nazca in 1975 by the International Explorers Society; Briton Julian Nott piloted *Condor I* to 300 feet.

The Middle Ages in Europe saw the amazing Tower Jumpers, men of consummate faith who leapt from monastic towers and battlements in their attempts to fly. An early and relatively successful jumper was one Eilmer of Malmesbury, an English monk of the eleventh century. Chronicles of the time record him as travelling an eighth of a mile in his voluminous capes and cloaks before hitting the ground. The reports do not say whether his faith was as damaged by the fall as was his body — he was crippled for life.

In the thirteenth century, as western civilisation struggled out of the Dark Ages, the first serious treatise on manned flight was written by the gifted English scientist Sir Roger Bacon. He argued that flight was definitely practicable, proposing that objects could not only float in water but could also float in air, and he experimented with hollow globes. Unfortunately this work was not published for a further three hundred years.

Later that century in Cathay, Marco Polo became the first European to witness the flying of manned kites. Before a ship put to sea a special kite was often flown with an unlucky peasant attached. If the kite stayed up, the winds were construed as favourable: if it crashed, it was deemed best to postpone the voyage. In populous Cathay there were many peasants.

▲ *Another early attempt to fly was made by King Bladud, the so-called Flying King of Britain. Despite using all his wings, Bladud 'fell down upon the Temple of Apollo'.* Royal Aeronautical Society
▶ *The first recorded free flight by human beings.*
M. Pilâtre de Rozier and Major d'Arlandes leave terra firma on 21 November 1783. Marie-Hélène Reynaud/Canson & Montgolfier Museum
◀ Previous page: *The Nazca Indian balloon replica,* Condor 1. *Was this how a human being first went aloft?* Jim Woodman

Yet perhaps the most brilliant scientist of them all was Sir Isaac Newton, a man working in realms fantastic for his time. In 1686 he finished his *Philosophiae Naturalis Principia Mathematica*, an astounding work in which he propounded the physical laws controlling the flight of artifical satellites in space — three hundred years before the first satellite was launched. However, exponents of heavier-than-air flight were sorely discouraged by Sir Isaac's discoveries about gravity, his apple demonstrating conclusively that objects fell down from, and not up into, the air. So it was that people turned their attention elsewhere, and in 1670 Francesco Lana de Terzia, a Jesuit priest of Italy, proposed that development should concentrate on lighter-than-air flight.

This initiative was pursued in the early 1700s by another priest, Father Bartholomeu Laurenco de Gusmão of Portugal. He devised the *Passarola* — 'giant bird' — in which he incorporated a large boat-like gondola, a sail, and several large copper globes containing magnets. The air was somehow to be sucked out of the globes and the contraption would rise into the air. This flying machine was built but, fortunately for the pilot, no attempt to fly it was ever made.

However, the good Father did demonstrate the principle of lighter-than-air flight to the court of Portugal. He attached a silken bag to a small tray of burning paper and King John V and his startled courtiers watched it rise to the lofty ceiling. The story has it that a footman stamped the tiny balloon to pieces when it set some curtains alight, and that was that. De Gusmão went no further with balloons, but one report alleges that while he was in the Portuguese colony of Brazil he flew a bird-like glider from one side of a valley to the other. This report is not proven, but there now seemed little doubt that, in tandem with the scientific discoveries of eighteenth-century Europe, it was only a matter of time before humanity finally cast loose its earthly bonds.

In Britain in 1750 the first dedicated rocket, the *A3*, reached an altitude of about 4,000 feet from a launching on the outskirts of London. In 1776 Henry Cavendish identified the gas hydrogen and proved it was both combustible and lighter than air. In France Joseph Montgolfier followed this discovery by attemping to contain hydrogen in a canopy and so lift objects into the air. A paper manufacturer, Montgolfier couldn't find a material that was impervious to the gas and so abandoned this line of experiment. But he had also been intrigued that paper was carried up a chimney by smoke from a fire and, in 1782, with his brother Etienne, he filled an upturned silk bag with smoke and watched it rise to the ceiling. Unlike Father de Gusmão, however, the brothers experimented further, using larger and

◀ *This flying machine was not far removed from the witch's broomstick theory of flight.* David Partridge/Air 2 Air

▼ *June 1783, and the Montgolfier brothers launch their un-manned hot air ballon at Annonay en Vivarais.* Marie-Hélène Reynaud/ Canson & Montgolfier Museum

larger containers and canopies. But, as is the case with many steps into the unknown, the Montgolfiers quite wrongly concluded that it was the smoke itself — rather than the heat — that contained this amazing property of lift.

On 4 June 1783, at their paper factory at Annonay near Lyons, they filled a 38-foot-diameter linen balloon with smoke from a fire of straw and released it. The balloon rose to an estimated 6,000 feet, and after ten minutes landed 1½ miles away. This short flight caused a sensation in the scientific centres of Britain and France, but more was to come.

◀ *M. Joseph Montgolfier et . . .* Marie-Hélène Reynaud/Canson & Montgolfier Museum
▼ *. . . M. Etienne Montgolfier.* Marie-Hélène Reynaud/Canson & Montgolfier Museum

E. MONGOLFIER.

On 27 August near Paris, French physicist Jacques Charles filled a 13-foot-diameter balloon with hydrogen gas and released it. The Académie Française had solved the problem of the porosity of the balloon fabric by lining the inside of the silk canopy with rubber. The small balloon rose to about 3,000 feet and stayed aloft for a remarkable three-quarters of an hour. Unfortunately it landed 15 miles away and the local peasantry, thinking it a monster from the skies, attacked and destroyed it with their pitchforks. Despite this unforeseen loss, the race was now on to make the first manned flight.

At the Château de Versailles on 9 September, before King Louis XVI and Marie Antoinette, the Montgolfiers launched a 74-foot-high hot air balloon of rag paper reinforced with linen. But as no one was sure what would happen to a man when he went up into the sky, in a fore-runner of the first space flights using mice and dogs, this 'Montgolfière' carried into the firmament in a wicker cage a cockerel, a duck and a sheep. It flew for eight minutes and landed 1½ miles away. The country of cordon bleu cuisine pronounced the birds still edible and therefore suffering no ill effects from their amazing experience. Marie Antoinette installed the flying sheep in her private zoo.

In a train of thought akin to that of the earlier Chinese kite fliers, Louis XVI decreed that the first man to fly should be a criminal from the Bastille — if he were lost it would be of no consequence. The French nobility were aghast that the human conquest of the air should be left to a convict — and a commoner, to boot — so Monsieur Jean-François Pilâtre de Rozier volunteered for the honour with his friend, Major (later Marquis) François d'Arlandes.

From another Montgolfière, this time 78 feet high, a gallery was suspended. Still believing that it was the smoke that had the property of lift, a foul-smelling fire of old shoes, wet kindling, straw and rotten meat was prepared in the grounds of the Château la Muette in the Bois de Boulogne. As well as the King and Queen of France, an extraordinarily large crowd gathered on 21 November 1783. The Major and Monsieur de Rozier stepped into opposite sides of the gallery, clouds of black smoke billowed upwards to fill the paper and linen canopy, and the tethering lines were cast off.

The blue and gold Montgolfière rose slowly above the château and the cheering crowd, drifted over the rooftops of Paris at about 500 feet for twenty-five minutes, and landed safely 5½ miles away on the Butte-aux-Cailles. It was the first confirmed flight by human beings, and de Rozier and d'Arlandes were the first aeronauts.

eighteenth century. In a gaily coloured red and white striped balloon contained within a netting, Charles and Robert flew 25 miles to Nesle-la-Vallee in only two hours.

The scientific explanation of lighter-than-air flight is that 'when a gas less dense than air is enclosed in a container, the difference between the density of the gas and the air it displaces causes the container to rise'. This applies equally to hot air, which is less dense than cold air, and to hydrogen. The irony is that Archimedes discovered this law of physics in the third century BC. It had taken the human race 2,000 years to learn how to apply it in order to fly, but now that flight had been achieved events progressed quickly.

◄ *In August, Charles launched the first hydrogen balloon from the Champs de Mars.* Marie-Helene Reynaud/Canson & Montgolfier Museum

▼ *Before King Louis XVI, a duck, a cockerel and a sheep took to the skies in September 1783.* Marie-Hélène Reynaud/Canson & Montgolfier Museum

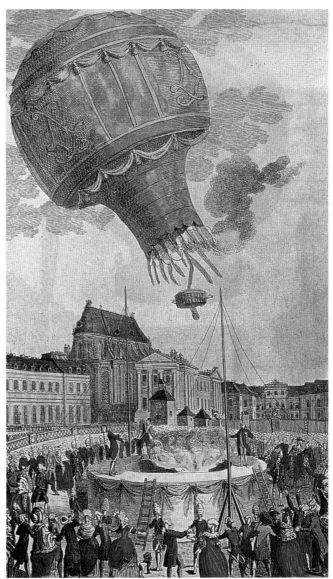

'It is the sport of the gods!' declared Marie Antoinette who, a few years later, was beheaded by the same Parisian mob that had cheered that first flight with her. Other enthusiasts claimed that 'journeys by air will be so speedy, so convenient, and so low in cost we shall see even women visiting the far corners of the earth'. And a more romantic Gallic view was of clandestine meetings where 'the lover will fly onto the roof of his mistress's house, leaving the machine there ready for a quicker departure'. The era of flight was born.

Only ten days later in the Tuileries, before another huge crowd, and with Joseph Montfgolfier as guest of honour, Jacques Charles and Aine Robert made the first flight in a gas balloon. Contemporary reports estimated the crowd at 400,000, an immense gathering for the

▲ *Charles and Robert follow with the first gas balloon flight on 1 December 1783. Here, Charles is alone in the basket after Robert had stepped out.* Marie-Hélène Reynaud/Canson & Montgolfier Museum

The first flight outside France was in Britain nine months later, on 15 September 1784, when Italian Vincenzo Lunardi took off from the grounds of the Honourable Artillery Company near Moorfields in London in a hydrogen balloon, with a dog, a cat, a pigeon, and a bottle of wine. The bottle of wine, or, more usually, one of champagne, was becoming mandatory as well as traditional. Balloons were apt to land anywhere, and many a farmer and vintner had to be placated with a glass or two of bubbly after surveying the resultant damage to his crops. Lunardi landed his cat at North Mimms after it became cold, but then flew on to Long Mead in Hertfordshire, a flight of 24 miles in a little over two hours.

A rare instance of early Anglo-French co-operation took place on 5 January 1785, when Dr John Jeffries and Jean-Pierre Blanchard took off from Dover in a cold north-west breeze to attempt to cross the English Channel. The flight was touch and go, but by jettisoning all non-essentials — including Monsieur Blanchard's trousers — the gas balloon landed 12 miles inland from Calais, completing the first aerial crossing of the Channel and the first international flight.

On 15 June, Pilâtre de Rozier and Jules de Romain attempted a crossing in the opposite direction, from Boulogne-sur-la-mer to England. An often quoted reason for this difficult flight against the prevailing winds was the rivalry between de Rozier and Blanchard, but de Rozier had another reason for visiting England — a love affair with a young English rose, Miss d'Ayer. But he and Romain weren't so fortunate as Blanchard and Jeffries. They were experimenting with a combined hot air and hydrogen balloon, the *Tour de Calais*, and the highly inflammable gas caught fire and the balloon crashed. De Rozier, the first aeronaut, and his friend were killed in the first air crash. Another fatality was narrowly averted when Major John Money took off from Norwich and was blown off course over the North Sea. He came down 20 miles off Great Yarmouth but, with the water up to his chin as the balloon sank beneath him, was rescued by a revenue cutter.

Flying was all the rage in Britain and Europe, but as well as entertainment and sport many scientific studies and experiments were carried out by balloons, or aerostats, as they came to be called. The eighteenth century was a period of extensive geographical and scientific study, and in August 1785 one of the greatest expeditions left Brest under the command of the Comte de la Pérouse. He took with him two frigates, the *Astrolabe* and the *Boussole*, the most experienced scientists of France, the most advanced instruments — even including contributions from arch-enemy Britain — and several 'small aerostatic balloons' to study the winds of the upper air. In South America la Pérouse reported that 'they amused the Chileans'. If not the first balloons over that continent (if that honour is given to the Nazca Indians) la Pérouse was certainly the first European to fly balloons there. He was believed to have flown the small aerostats from the Great Barrier Reef, so the first balloon flight in Australia could have been as early as May 1788.

Some early flights were bizarre, and purely exhibitionistic. In 1789, at Meudon in France, Pierre Jetu Brisy flew a cylindrical hydrogen balloon whilst mounted on his horse on a platform hanging beneath. Other animal ascents followed, including one with a stag. In January 1793 Blanchard, first across the Channel, first to fly over Berlin, and first to make a successful parachute jump, sailed to North America and introduced the joys of flight to that continent.

Inevitably, the new playthings were adapted for warfare. The French general Morlot, in 1794, directed the Battle of Fleuris against combined Austrian and Dutch forces from a hydrogen balloon and gained a resounding victory.

The highly inflammable but easier to inflate hydrogen balloons, or Charlières, were taking over from the cumbersome and larger hot air Montgolfières, but whichever type was flown, the early aeronauts frequently diced with death. Blanchard himself died in 1809 from the effects of a heart attack he had suffered while flying the previous year. James Sadler and his balloon came down in the Bristol Channel off Llandudno in 1812 while attempting to cross the Irish Sea, and in 1819 in Paris the first woman aeronaut was killed. Madame Madeleine Blanchard, wife of Jean-Pierre, was giving an aerial firework display when her balloon caught fire and crashed onto a roof. Madeleine was tipped out of the basket, fell to the street below and broke her neck. And Thomas Harris, inventor of the first valve to empty a balloon canopy of gas or hot air and so reduce the amount of drag on landing, died in 1824 in an affair of the heart. He had taken a girlfriend for a joy ride, pulled the valve cord by mistake, and crashed into an oak tree near Croydon, south of London. A *liaison dangereuse* indeed.

Spurred on by the successes of lighter-than-air flight, scientists and adventurers delved once again into the mysteries of heavier-than-air flight. The breakthrough

▲ *M. Blanchard and Dr Jeffries cross the English Channel in a hydrogen balloon. The rudder and wings look impressive, but helped not the slightest.* Royal Aeronautical Society

◄ *An impression of the* Tour de Calais *of de Rozier and Romain, just before disaster struck over Boulogne-sur-mer.* Royal Aeronautical Society

was made in 1809 by a baronet of Yorkshire, Sir George Cayley. He has become known as the 'father of aerial navigation'. He established the principles of the curved aerofoil section — the aeroplane wing — upon which heavier-than-air flight relies for its lift. In 1849 he built a glider strong enough to carry a small boy and, in 1853, a much larger glider which flew his reluctant coachman a considerable distance.

The next step was to provide a power source, an engine of some description, so as to be able to fly at will. This desire applied equally to balloonists; they, too, were looking for an engine in order to steer their wind-directed craft. Paddles, sails, oars and rudders had all been tried, but to no avail.

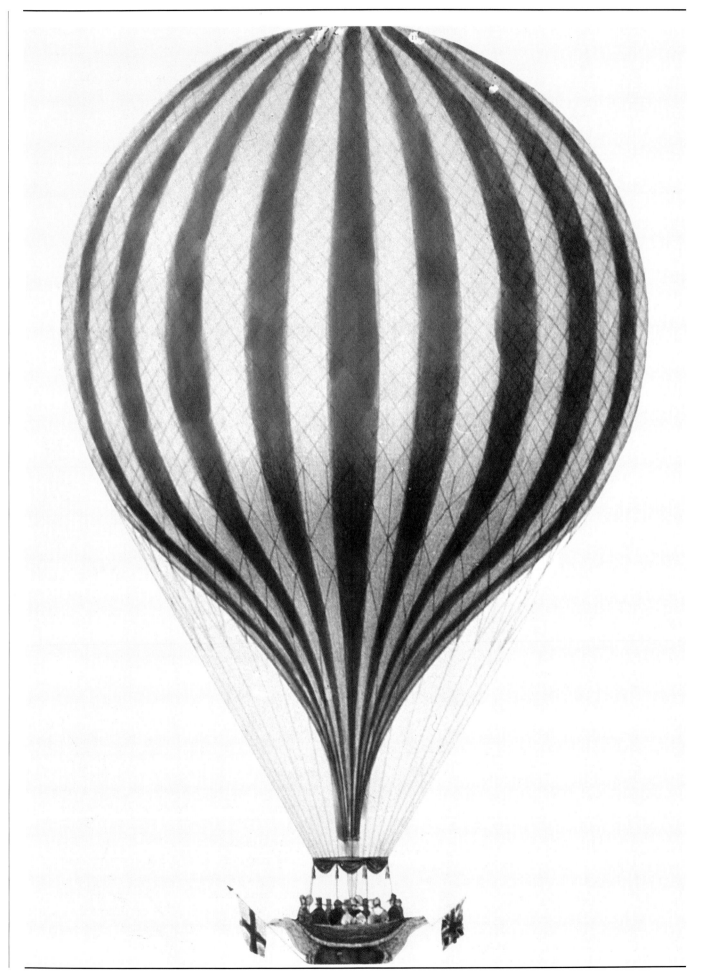

▲ *Nadar's* Le Geant *narrowly avoids a train during its wild passage across Hanover in 1863.* Royal Aeronautical Society
◄ *Charles Green's* Royal Vauxhall *hydrogen balloon. Green made 500 flights before retiring, and proposed the first trans-Atlantic crossing using the prevailing westerly winds at 10,000 feet.* Royal Aeronautical Society

One of the longest early flights was made in November 1836, when Charles Green and two passengers took off from the Vauxhall Gardens in London in the *Royal Vauxhall*, a hydrogen balloon made of 6,000 feet of crimson and white silk. They crossed the Channel that evening, and supper was served by lamplight above the deep red glow of the iron foundries of Liège. After a chilly night, and at an altitude of 12,000 feet, they saw the sun rise over Poland while those below were still in

► *Sir George Cayley, baronet of Yorkshire, the father of heavier-than-air flight.* Royal Aeronautical Society

darkness. The *Royal Vauxhall* finally landed at Weilsburg in the German Duchy of Nassau after an eighteen-hour flight of 480 miles. Green went on to make five hundred flights before he retired.

The balloon continued to be adapted for various uses, primarily military, and in 1849 the first air raid took place at the siege of Venice. The encircling Austrian Army launched a fleet of hot air balloons, each with a 30-pound bomb on board to be released by a time-delay fuse. Fortunately for the Venetians the wind changed direction, and although the bombs caused some alarm there were no casualties. The first powered balloon was flown by Frenchman Henri Gifford in 1852, using a steam engine driving a windmill paddle, but in anything other than still air the balloon was still subject to the winds. During the American Civil War tethered balloons were flown for artillery spotting and direction, and in 1861 the Union forces towed a balloon by barge along the Potomac River to observe the Confederate forces on the opposite bank.

The greatest balloon of them all was *Le Geant*, launched in 1863 by Monsieur Nadar. The whole affair stood 186 feet high, with a carriage beneath measuring 20 feet high and 15 feet wide, something like a small bungalow divided into six compartments. This massive aerostat was designed to lift up to 4½ tons. *Le Geant* lifted off from Paris on 18 October with six people on board and flew westward in a rising wind. It landed near Hanover in a near-gale but did not stop there. The huge envelope dragged the compartment cross-country at something like 30 miles per hour, leaving a swathe of wreckage and injured passengers across the land and even across a railway line before it finally came to rest. But there was romance as well as drama in the skies. A couple were actually married in a balloon high above New York in 1865 — nearer my God to thee.

Ballooning and the search for dirigibility — the ability to steer the aircraft — became a major quest of the nineteenth century, and in 1866 the first aviation society was formed. It was the Aeronautical Society of Great Britain (now the Royal Aeronautical Society) and in 1868 the first aircraft show was held at the Crystal Palace, south of London.

A glimpse of the vast possibilities of aviation was provided during the Franco-Prussian War in 1870. Paris was besieged and effectively isolated from the rest of the world by the enemy, so the Parisians built hydrogen balloons — sixty-six of them — to regain contact. The aerostats were constructed in the then disused railway stations, and most of them were launched at night to avoid target practice by the surrounding Prussians. Of the sixty-six launched, fifty-six landed in friendly territory, the *Ville d'Orléans* carrying two people as far away as Telemark in Norway. All told, these balloons carried 2½ million letters and newspaper reports, one-hundred-and-two people, five dogs and four hundred carrier pigeons for return messages. One balloon, the *Jacquard*, carried a prince away from the siege. 'Now I begin the greatest trip of my life,' he is reported to have said. 'This air voyage will be talked about everywhere.' It was. The balloon lifted off from Paris, soared over Maine-et-Loire and Brittany and out over the Atlantic Ocean. The prince was never seen again.

On 9 August 1884, the hydrogen aerostat *La France* completed a circular flight of 5 miles, taking off from Chalais-Meudon and returning to the same point after twenty-three minutes aloft. This first controlled flight used an electric motor that drove a 23-foot propeller, giving this first 'dirigible' an air speed of about 14 miles per hour in light airs.

The beginning of the twentieth century saw all the hurdles to heavier-than-air flight crossed; it was now only a matter of time before someone, somewhere, put all the pieces together in the right order.

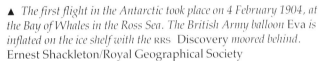

▲ *The first flight in the Antarctic took place on 4 February 1904, at the Bay of Whales in the Ross Sea. The British Army balloon* Eva *is inflated on the ice shelf with the* RRS Discovery *moored behind.* Ernest Shackleton/Royal Geographical Society

◄ *Sir Hiram Maxim's amazing 104-foot wingspan* Leviathan *of the 1890s. It became airborne within the limits of its guard rails, but developed so much lift it almost tore the whole apparatus apart when it took off.* Royal Aeronautical Society

▼ *The first aerial photograph of Antarctica, taken from* Eva *looking down upon the Ross Ice Shelf.* Ernest Shackleton/Royal Geographical Society

Away in Kitty Hawk in North Carolina Wilbur and Orville Wright had built a box-like machine they called *Flyer*. It was powered by a weak petrol engine, was launched by a catapult, and had no wheels. On December 17, 1903, in the best of three take-offs that day, *Flyer* travelled 852 feet in 59 seconds at a height of between 8 and 12 feet. The first sustained, manned, powered and controlled heavier-than-air flight had at last taken place, though not without a little controversy.

Richard Pearse of New Zealand had reportedly flown his 25-foot wingspan tricycle undercarriage aeroplane for nearly a quarter of a mile in March 1902. Four other flights followed in 1903 near Christchurch in South Island, including one on Easter Saturday of about five-eighths of a mile before landing in the Opihi River bed. Although witnessed, without the publicity and official announcements of Kitty Hawk no-one outside New Zealand knew of these flights.

But still balloons were making pioneer flights, even to the ends of the Earth. The first balloon over the Antarctic was flown by the explorer Lieutenant Robert Falcon Scott, Royal Navy, in February 1904, from the Bay of Whales in the Ross Sea. It was a tethered flight during the 1900–04 expedition, and *Eva* ascended to 800 feet.

Scott, a seaman, thought the wicker basket 'very inadequate'. Ernest Shackleton next ascended and took the first aerial photographs of the continent.

By now, hot air ballooning had all but disappeared, except among a few enthusiasts in Europe, but gas ballooning continued both as an entertainment and a strategic option. In Germany Count von Zeppelin had developed his large dirigible airships, and during the First World War these Zeppelins flew more than fifty bombing raids to London and other towns along the east coast of Britain. The vulnerability of the airship was exposed as soon as viable fighter aeroplanes like the

▲ *The little-known Richard Pearse of New Zealand. Did he make the first aeroplane flight?* Museum of Transport & Technology, Auckland

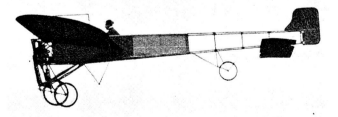

▲ *124 years after a balloon first crossed the English Channel, Louis Blériot crosses from France to England in 1909. After his success he received more than one hundred orders for this Type XI monoplane.* Royal Aeronautical Society

◄ *Pearse's 1902 aeroplane, reconstructed from his drawings and parts salvaged from the original aeroplane.* Museum of Transport & Technology, Auckland

Sopwith Camel were produced, and balloons were once again relegated to observing artillery and troop movements along the Western Front. The Royal Navy, however, still found them effective as aerial escorts and submarine spotters for slow-moving convoys at sea.

After the 'war to end all wars' both aeroplane and balloon development were directed towards more peaceful ends. Aerial mail services sprang up around the world, and the Daily Mail newspaper of Britain put up prize money for the first non-stop flight across the North Atlantic. They offered £10,000, a princely sum in those days of post-war uncertainty.

The response was immediate and flyers began planning crossings from west to east to take advantage of the prevailing winds. On 14 June, 1919, Captain John Alcock and Lieutenant Arthur Whitton Brown of Britain took off from St John's in Newfoundland in a converted Vickers Vimy bomber. This massive bi-plane, powered by twin Rolls Royce Eagle engines, made the first non-stop aerial crossing of the Atlantic, ending its 16½-hour flight with a landing in a bog at Clifden in Ireland.

Yet lighter-than-air craft were still in the race. Just three weeks after Alcock and Brown the first balloon crossed on 6 July — and did it the 'wrong way', causing a world sensation. The Royal Air Force dirigible *R34* flew from East Fortune in Fife to New York to make the first east-west crossing against the prevailing winds. It took 108 sometimes terrifying hours, and R.G. Scott and his crew were greeted as heroes in the United States. They then flew back to Pulham in East Anglia, and *R34* also became the first aircraft to cross in both directions.

The way had been opened for regular Atlantic crossings, and Britain and Germany vied for the greatest prestige. Germany was rewarded in 1929 when the *Graf Zeppelin* completed the first around-the-world flight, taking just three weeks and including one non-stop leg of 7,000 miles. Jules Verne's 'impossible' eighty days had been put firmly into perspective. Britain replied with the Vickers *R100* airship designed by the innovative Barnes Wallis, and it flew to Canada and back in style in 1930. Britain abandoned balloon development in favour of the aeroplane after the disaster of the maiden flight of *R101* to India. Forty-eight people died in a conflagration of hydrogen at Beauvais, in France, when the 5-million-cubic-foot airship crashed.

Still using the highly inflammable hydrogen, Germany's massive dirigibles now dominated the trans-Atlantic air routes — until 6 May 1937. The giant 200-ton *Hindenburg*, capable of speeds of 80 knots, had just completed its twenty-first Atlantic crossing and was coming in to land at Lakehurst in New Jersey. It's

▼ *The first non-stop aerial crossing of the Atlantic was made by this Vickers Vimy World War I bomber in 1919. Pilots Alcock and Brown were knighted for their achievement; a statue of the two men now stands outside the Queen's Building at Heathrow Airport.* Royal Aeronautical Society

▲ *The RAF airship R34, on loan from the Royal Navy, was the first lighter-than-air craft to cross the Atlantic, and the first aircraft to cross both ways. Before landing at Long Island, Squadron Leader Pritchard parachuted down to supervise the landing operations.* Royal Aeronautical Society

▲ *All that remained of the British* R101 *airship at Beauvais in France. Major Scott, commander of the earlier* R34, *died in the disaster.* Royal Aeronautical Society

▼ *The German* Hindenburg *exploded into flame as it attempted to come alongside the mooring mast at Lakehurst. Was it an accident or was it sabotage?* Royal Aeronautical Society

probable that a strike of static electricity from the steel mooring tower flashed into the balloon, and the greatest airship of them all burst into flames. The hydrogen burned fiercely, completely destroying the aircraft and killing thirty-five of its ninety-seven crew and passengers. The propaganda machine of Nazi Germany mumbled dark allegations of sabotage, but hydrogen balloons were disasters waiting to happen. The *Hindenburg* and the *R101* tragedies signalled the end of the commercial era of ballooning. However, sports gas-ballooning without engines continued through the Gordon Bennett Air Race, begun by the American publisher in 1906, and hydrogen began to be replaced by the far more expensive but inert helium gas, first used in the 1930s in America.

Lighter-than-air flight appeared doomed to languish while heavier-than-air development flourished, spurred on by the advent of the Second World War. In Britain Sir Frank Whittle invented the jet engine, the first jet aeroplanes flew in Germany and Britain, and the first long-range rockets were launched from Germany. Yet balloons still had their moments of glory, and during the Battle of Britain more than two thousand four hun-

▲ *Barrage balloons moored above London during the Blitz in 1940.*
Royal Aeronautical Society
▶ *The first jet airliner, the de Havilland Comet, here in* BOAC *livery.*
Later models are now used for marine surveillance under the name of
Nimrod. Royal Aeronautical Society

dred gas barrage balloons were tethered over the bombed and beleaguered islands. The British joked that if the balloons were cut away the country would sink. Balloons were again used for convoy protection, and also over the D-Day invasion fleet and the beach-heads of Normandy in 1944.

But their strangest use was the bizarre balloon offensive begun by the Japanese high command in November 1944. More than nine thousand unmanned hydrogen balloons, or *Fu-Gos*, were launched from Japan into the jet stream over the Pacific for bombing raids on North America. The *Fu-Gos* carried a payload of about 22 pounds of explosives and incendiaries fitted with time-delay mechanisms; the plan was to bomb and terrorise the western coast of America. The Allies also feared a biological warfare offensive by this method. Amazingly, four hundred *Fu-Gos* actually made the 6,000 mile flight and six people were killed, the only casualties from enemy action on mainland United States.

The balloon as a strategic option did return briefly after the Second World War, when Goodyear in the

United States developed gas dirigibles for submarine detection. Working in conjunction with aircraft carriers the balloons operated as anti-submarine hunter-killers, but were soon replaced by the more versatile helicopter. Blimps were also flown for coastal surveillance and as part of the first early warning system, the Dew (Distance Early Warning) Line that warned of any nuclear attack.

Development in flight returned once again to peaceful ends, and the first jet airliner — the sleek, streamlined de Havilland Comet — entered service in Britain on 2 May 1952. The first artificial satellite, the Russian *Sputnik I*, was launched into space on 4 October 1957; as it circled the Earth it could be seen from below as the metal reflected the Sun's rays. In another amazing example of unlikely British-French co-operation the BAC/ Aérospatiale Concorde, the first supersonic airliner, took to the skies on 2 March, 1967. Ballooning was reserved once again for upper atmosphere research, weather forecasting, periodic altitude record attempts and scientific research.

▼ *Edward Yost, whose propane burner revolutionised hot air*
ballooning in the 1960s. He is still flying. Balloon Aloft

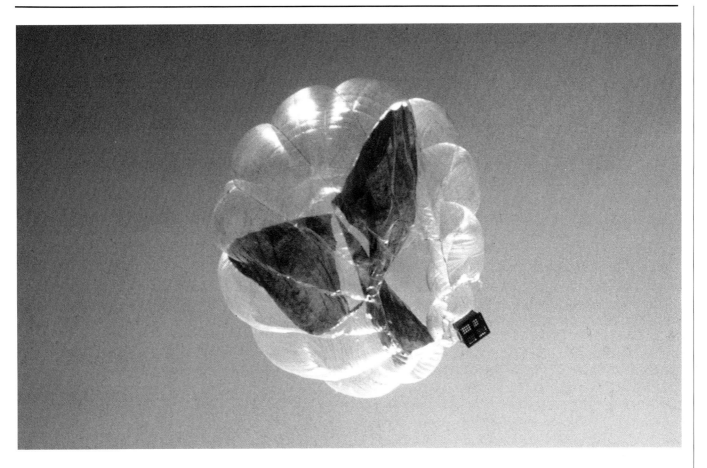

On 16 August 1960, Captain Joseph Kittinger of the United States Air Force made a helium balloon ascent to 102,800 feet — nearly 20 miles up from the Earth. A little later, Major Simons broke the 20-mile barrier with an ascent to 105,000 feet. On 12 April 1961, cosmonaut Major Yuri Gagarin of the Soviet Union made the first manned flight into space with a 25,394½-mile orbit of the Earth in *Vostok I*.

Only eight years later, in 1969, humanity took its first steps upon the surface of another planet. Americans Neil Armstrong and Edwin Aldrin landed on the moon in the lunar module *Eagle* on 21 July, making that 'giant step for Mankind'.

It was in the United States that the revival of hot air ballooning was made possible. A former space and high-altitude balloon engineer, Edward Yost, developed a practical air heater powered by propane, the safe and efficient gas used in camping and yacht stoves. Yost flew a hot-air balloon using the new heating system on 10 October 1960 at Bruning in Nebraska; it was a success. Suddenly lighter-than-air flight was interesting again — and cheap. Using the new non-rip nylon, gaily coloured aerostats once more appeared in the sky. Yost and veteran balloonist Don Piccard took the heater invention to Britain in 1963, and in *Channel Champ* made the first hot air balloon crossing of the Channel in late March. American physicist Tracy Barnes further developed Yost's propane burner system, and by 1971 had

▲ *The first purpose-built solar-powered balloon, manufactured by Dominic Michealis in 1972. The outer envelope was made of Melinex polyester film just 6 microns thick, and contained a trefoil heat collector. The balloon carried a man in tethered flight.* Dominic Michealis

also introduced a parachute-style venting system for envelopes. By 1973 interest had increased to the extent that the first World Hot Air Balloon Championship was held in Albuquerque in New Mexico; sixty aerostats competed. It was a fitting tribute to Edward Yost, the father of modern hot air ballooning.

In all, 1973 was a busy year. The first solar-powered hot air balloon took to the air. Designed by Barnes — it was not the first such balloon to be made; that honour goes to Dominic Michealis of Britain — the 220,000-cubic-foot black envelope rose into the skies over Charlotte in North Carolina. That same year the first airship inflated with hot air and not gas made its maiden flight at the Icicle Balloon meet in January at Newbury in Berkshire. Inventor Don Cameron circled his D-96 hot air airship over the balloons below, stopped it, flew it into the breeze and then landed.

The surviving gas balloonists naturally took to hot air flying too, and through the 1970s and 1980s records and challenges in both areas came under assault. In 1978, in the eleventh attempt of that decade, Americans Ben Abruzzo, Max Anderson and Larry Newman flew the

Atlantic in the helium balloon *Double Eagle II*. Abruzzo, Anderson and Newman took off from Maine and 137 hours later landed in a Normandy wheatfield near Misery, though they said the flight was anything but that. Two years later Anderson and his son Kristian made the first non-stop trans-America flight in the helium balloon *Kitty Hawk*. Joe Kittinger completed the first solo trans-Atlantic crossing in 1984, also from Maine, but *Rosie O'Grady* was going so well when it crossed the European coast that he continued on to Italy and an audience in the Vatican.

After a gap of forty-one years, caused by the Second World War, gas ballooning meets began again with the reintroduction of the Gordon Bennett Trophy in 1979. Eighteen helium balloons inflated at Long Beach in California, and the event was won by Abruzzo and Anderson in *Double Eagle III* with a flight of 583 miles eastwards into Colorado. The English Channel returned to the news in 1981 when the first solar-powered hot air balloon crossed from England to France on 21 August. Dominic Michealis was the designer and Julian Nott the pilot. Fortunately they chose a sunny day.

Aeroplane 'firsts' continued to be achieved, though some might say that some of the firsts were almost a step backwards. After centuries of leaping, running, flapping and pedalling, man-powered flight had finally been achieved. The *Prix Peugeot*, for a man-powered flight of more than 33 feet, had first been offered in 1912 but it was not taken until July 1921 at the Longchamps Racecourse in Paris. Gabriel Poulain from the Channel Islands was the pilot, madly pedalling a bicycle with wings he called *Aviette*. He flew 40 feet. Other developments were made in man-powered flight around the world, notably in Germany and Japan, and at Southampton University in Britain.

▼ *The* Gossamer Albatross *flying above the English Channel. It completed the first man-powered aerial crossing in June 1979.* Royal Aeronautical Society

In the mid-1970s a British–American team — the Gossamer Squadron — took up the challenge of man-powered flight in earnest, and in England, on 23 August 1977, Bryan Allen pedalled the *Gossamer Condor* 1.35 miles over a figure-of-eight course to win the £50,000 Kremer Prize. The traditional hurdle of all flight, the English Channel, now beckoned. A new aeroplane was designed and built, and at dawn on 12 June 1979, Bryan Allen and *Gossamer Albatross* took off from Folkestone for France. At times flying only a foot above the waves, Allen kept on pedalling to the point of exhaustion, and landed on the beach at Cap Gris-Nez after a 2-hour, 49-minute flight of 22 nautical miles. This distance was bettered by Kanellas Kanellopoulos on 23 April 1988, when he pedalled *Daedalus* from Crete to Santorini, a distance of 72 miles.

In the more high-tech flying areas, the United States Air Force *Voyager* became, in December 1986, the first aircraft to fly non-stop around the world. Flown by Richard Rutan and Jeana Yeager from Edwards Air Force Base in California, *Voyager* took 9 days 3 minutes and 44 seconds to complete a 29,986.665 mile aerial circumnavigation of the Earth. And in April 1989, a British Airways Concorde completed the first supersonic flight around the world, claiming twelve new

speed records in its circumnavigation westward from Heathrow Airport.

Ballooning is also now high-tech, and one of the latest records to fall was the first non-stop Atlantic crossing by a hot-air balloon. Per Lindstrand and Richard Branson of Britain flew from Maine and landed on 3 July 1987, albeit briefly, at Limavady in Northern Ireland. *Virgin Flyer's* envelope incorporated an aluminium-Melinex film on nylon, while the capsule was of aluminium pressurised by a super-charged piston engine. This is worlds away from the rag-paper and open gallery of a Montgolfière, but there is still a place for romance in modern ballooning.

On the night of 15 September 1979, in a small clearing deep in the Forest of Thuringisan in East Germany, eight people as quietly as possible inflated a hot air balloon. The Wetzel and Strelczyk families of Poessnek had decided to flee to the west across the Iron Curtain.

At 0240 hours they lifted off in their makeshift balloon, climbed to almost 8,000 feet as the border guards began hunting for them in the sky with powerful searchlights, and landed half an hour later in West Germany. The balloon was completely home made, the envelope being sewn together in the cellar of the Strelczyks' house, while the basket was simply a wooden platform

▲ *Boarding one's motor yacht, Mediterranean style.* Sally Samins

▲ *Concorde, the first supersonic airliner, here in British Airways livery high above the North Atlantic. Plans for further supersonic airliners are afoot in Britain and in the United States.* British Airways

with the gas cylinders roped together in the middle. It was grass-roots flying again, and de Rozier and d'Arlandes would have been equally at home in this aerostat as they were for the first flight in 1783.

THE RECORD BREAKERS

THE FIRST HURDLE

*T*HE FIRST international hurdle of flight has traditionally been the crossing of the English Channel, but recorded crossings of the Channel from France to England have happened on only two occasions, in both of which hydrogen balloons were used.

In 1906, in the inaugural Gordon Bennett Air Race, sixteen gas balloons lifted off from the Tuileries in Paris on 30 September. The wind was from the east-south-east at first, but after the balloons were airborne it veered to the south and the fleet was blown towards the English Channel. Nine of the pilots elected to land in France but the remaining seven decided to keep flying northwards. Amongst these were American cavalry lieutenant Frank Lahm and his assistant, Major Henry Hersey, in the balloon *United States*. They won the trophy with a flight of 22 hours to Fylinghall near Whitby in Yorkshire, crossing the Channel and much of the length of England in a marathon 395 miles. The other six balloons also made successful crossings.

The other crossing of the Channel was by the pioneer French balloonist Charles Dollfus, also in an early Gordon Bennett Race. His balloon was blown across to Wales over which he arrived at night in a high wind. His major problem was landing, and he decided to come down into a forest and destroy the envelope, the only sure way of stopping the balloon quickly. Dollfus survived this, and the Second World War, to continue ballooning into the 1970s before he died.

The first hot air balloon didn't cross until 1963, when Americans Edward Yost and Don Piccard planned an attempt with the help of British balloonist Anthony Smith. They flew a Raven balloon of 60,000 cubic feet heated by Yost's innovative propane burner, and crossed at about 13,000 feet. The record flight took 3 hours and 7 minutes, and Yost and Piccard landed in France near the Belgian border: they christened the balloon *Channel Champ*.

◄ Previous page: *The English Channel as few seamen know it — a placid blue washing the foot of its famous white cliffs.* Jerry Young/ Katz Eyes
▼ *The 1981 solar balloon, flown across the English Channel by Julian Nott from Dover to Calais.* Dominic Michealis

The English Channel also has another name. The French call it the Sleeve (*La Manche*), and this deceptively narrow stretch of water has now been flown over by almost every sort of aerial machine, including hang gliders launched from balloons and a man-powered aircraft. One of the more interesting crossings took place in 1981 as part of the International Solar Energy Conference in Brighton, when Julian Nott of Britain flew a solar-powered hot air balloon to France.

The balloon was designed by Domenic Michealis, his third such balloon. This model incorporated two envelopes to create a greenhouse effect. The outer envelope was transparent, to concentrate the heat of the sun's rays, while the inner envelope was a standard black Cameron 104,000 cubic foot, to absorb the heat and transfer it to the air inside. For the Channel attempt the balloon was initially inflated using a propane burner, but once in shape all the lift was generated by the

▲ *After a break of 41 years the Gordon Bennett Race for gas balloons began again in 1979. The balloons inflate on the quay before the* RMS Queen Mary *at Long Beach in California.* Balloon Aloft

sun. It provided enough energy to take the balloon to 1,000 feet.

The Michealis Solar Balloon took off on 21 August at 0730 hours from South Barnham Farm in Kent, ten miles north-west of Dover. It was one of those rare English summer's days, so hot that a haze hangs over the green countryside. With ample lift provided by solar energy, Nott turned off the pilot flame completely and drifted across the blue Channel in silence. He remembers hearing the buzz of a hovercraft ferry, and even the beat and thump of the propellors of a tanker passing beneath. Nott used the burner just once during the flight, to steady his descent when he landed 10 miles south-east of Calais. The crossing took an hour and fifty minutes.

The adjacent, wider body of water of the North Sea was only conquered by balloon as recently as 1979, when Britons Simon Faithfull and Peter Morgan crossed this sadly polluted stretch of salt water. That was in a helium balloon; the first hot air balloon didn't cross until the summer of 1988 when Oliver Holmes, Richard Barr and John Derricott of Britain took off in a Thunder & Colt. They flew for just less than sixteen hours to complete the 425-mile flight across the grey sea that used to be called the German Ocean.

TRANS-ATLANTIC

After the English Channel the North Atlantic is the next traditional aeronautical challenge. When the Channel was first crossed in 1784, George Washington was reported to have said, in a reference to Lafayette: 'Our friends in Paris will now come flying through the air instead of ploughing the ocean.' His prediction was a little premature.

Following his successful 380-mile flight from Britain to Germany in 1836, Charles Green propounded an Atlantic crossing from west to east at about 10,000 feet. He had found a constant west to east air flow at this altitude, but he couldn't find any investors willing to support such an attempt. In 1844 Edgar Allan Poe wrote in the *New York Sun* that the first trans-Atlantic flight had been achieved, taking only three days and from east to west no less. It was a hoax. In 1859 John Wise of America put forward the theory that winds at very high altitudes are constant in direction and strength, and could be used for trans-oceanic flights. He was referring to the jet stream, and called it the 'rivers in the sky'. Wise built the hydrogen balloon *Atlantic* to test his theories, and it flew 1,200 miles from St Louis to Ontario. However, despite lengthy preparations, he never attempted the Atlantic.

The first serious attempt didn't come until 1910, when Walter Wellman's airship *America* left Atlantic City on 15 October, destination Europe. This 228-foot-long aircraft carried six men, a kitten, a radio, and was propelled by two internal combustion engines. One engine soon broke down, but the other took *America* 1,000 miles out over the North Atlantic before it, too, broke down. The airship ditched, and the crew and the kitten were rescued by a British steamer. The radio messages exchanged were the first ever sea-to-air radio communications. Britons Alcock and Brown were the first to fly the Atlantic non-stop: the Royal Air Force *R34* airship made the first east-west and double crossing: and American Charles Lindberg completed the first solo crossing in May 1927 in the *Spirit of St Louis*. The first balloon attempt finally came in 1958, when a British team took off from Tenerife in the Canaries on the evening of 12 December for an east-west crossing.

The Small World was a gondola-cum-boat helium balloon, and was designed by yachtsman and boat builder Colin Mudie. For crew he took his wife, Rosemary, and Arnold Eiloart and his son, Tim. Drawing on their experience as trans-Atlantic sailors they planned to fly across to the West Indies using the north-east trade winds, the same winds that sailing ships had been using since Columbus' voyage in 1492. *The Small World* flew a distance of 1,200 nautical miles in 94½ hours before running into heavy cumulo-nimbus clouds and storms. The balloon was being forced upwards and then downwards by colossal air pressures, and the crew kept venting helium to keep control of the balloon. 'It was like riding in a lift controlled by a mischievous child,' said Eiloart. When they had cleared the up-draughts they had to jettison all the ballast and non-essentials to keep the balloon in the air, but too much gas had gone. They were forced to drop clear of the envelope and ditch in mid-Atlantic. The gondola now reverted to a sailing boat, and they completed the remaining 1,450 miles to Barbados by sea, arriving safely on 5 January, 1959. *The Small World* was an inspired and innovative design that was to be copied for many later attempts.

The 1960s saw no attempts to cross the 'Pond', but after a lay period of eleven years the race was on again in earnest. In 1970 veteran British balloonist Malcolm Brighton tried his hand in *Free Life*, the first of the combined helium and hot air balloons. *Free Life* was built by Semco Balloons of America, and the American ballooning couple, the Andersons, accompanied Brighton on his west to east attempt on 20 September. They flew for 30 hours before being brought down by the weather southeast of Newfoundland, and that is the last known of them. No bodies or wreckage were ever found.

Three years later on 7 August 1973, another helium/hot air balloon with a gondola like *The Small World*'s lifted off from Maine. This balloon was called *Yankee Zephyr*, the pilot was Bobby Sparks, and he lasted only 23 hours before ditching in another storm. Sparks was rescued. The next to try was Thomas Gatch in *Light Heart* on 18 February, 1974. His was the first to attempt a high altitude crossing in the jet stream, utilising Wise's 'rivers in the sky'. *Light Heart* was in fact a cluster of ten super-pressure helium balloons — normally used for weather reporting — supporting the gondola beneath. The balloons were tried and tested, but Gatch disappeared into the Atlantic east of Bermuda. Again, no wreckage was ever found.

Less than a year later, on 6 January 1975, American balloonist Malcolm Forbes made the second high altitude attempt, but *Windborne* was uncontrollable even at

take-off and the balloon cluster had to be cut away before the flight had properly begun. On 21 August Bobby Sparks made his second attempt using the prevailing south-westerly low-altitude winds. This Semich balloon was called *Odyssey* but, despite its name, didn't travel far. With his chief ground crewman on board as a stowaway the flight lasted just two hours and five minutes after leaving Maine and Sparks splashed down once more into the ocean. *The Small World*-type gondola was recovered with its crew and the next year took to the air again under another Semich envelope as *Spirit of '76*. It was an American bicentennial attempt. Karl Thomas took off on 25 June 1976, from the old airship base at Lakehurst in New Jersey. Five hundred and fifty miles later Thomas was forced down by a storm and rescued by a Russian trawler.

Balloon mania was endemic this decade, and on 5 October, 1976, the seventh attempt at the Atlantic crossing lifted off from Maine. Hot air pioneer Edward Yost, flying the *Silver Fox* helium balloon that he had built himself, also used the low-altitude winds, and his progress was monitored daily at that year's Albuquerque Fiesta. Yost broke all the records set by *The Small World* eighteen years ago, and looked set fair to reach Europe when a change in wind defeated him. *Silver Fox* was being blown southwards and Yost was forced to ditch only 700 miles from Portugal in a flight that had originally taken him north of Newfoundland. He had flown 2,474 miles.

Yost then built another balloon, to be flown by fellow Americans Ben Abruzzo and Max Anderson on 9 September, 1977. *Double Eagle* broke Yost's new gas balloon distance record with a flight of 2,950 miles, but it all ended in the cold and stormy Denmark Strait between Iceland and Greenland. This flight lasted sixty-four hours, during which the balloon described a wide circle over the ocean south-east of Greenland. Abruzzo was suffering from exposure by this time, and actually had frostbite in his left foot. The two men and their gondola were rescued by helicopter and the ninth attempt rose into the air from Maine barely a month later on 10 October. Another Yost helium balloon of 86,000 cubic feet, *Eagle* was flown by Stevenson and Reinhard, but they took forty-six hours to fly only 220 miles before ditching in the face of a storm off Nova Scotia.

There was a breathing space of a year while teams on both sides of the Atlantic sought to learn the lessons from these nine unsuccessful attempts, and how to turn the weather that had defeated them into helping them. In Britain Don Cameron of Cameron Balloons built a combined helium/hot air balloon. Providing the lift was the inner helium gas envelope, while the outer surrounding envelope of hot air controlled by burners and vents would attempt to keep the gas at a steady tem-

◄ Double Eagle II *over the North Atlantic — destination Europe.* Ben Abruzzo

perature. This would obviate the need to vent any gas, and also provide a ballast system in place of heavy and cumbersome sand and water ballast. This balloon was called *Zanussi* after its major sponsor. Major Chris Davey of the British Army was co-pilot, and the launch was set for St. John's in Newfoundland. In July 1978, the team assembled in Canada, but a sudden illness delayed the take-off planned to coincide with a favourable weather system.

Meanwhile, further south in Maine in the United States, an American team was also in the final stages of an Atlantic attempt. Larry Newman had joined Abruzzo and Anderson in a Yost helium balloon using the gondola recovered from *Double Eagle*. The top half of this envelope was coated with silver to reflect the sun's heat

illness, and Cameron and Davey took off on the morning of 26 July, 1978, at 0720 hours, days later than they'd planned. All went well until the second day when, at 10,000 feet, the two men heard a sharp crack like a rifle shot reverberate through the balloon. The inner helium envelope had given way but, miraculously, they managed to keep control of the balloon and were able to continue flying. The inert helium gas seeped from the torn fabric but *Zanussi* struggled eastwards, her progress monitored as anxiously in Maine as in Britain.

The European coast came slowly closer, but by 29 July, the beginning of the third day, the wind had also become light and variable. The balloon was first pushed to the south and then north before finally approaching the Brittany coast from across the Bay of Biscay. On the

during the day, while the base below the equator was black to absorb the convected heat rising from the ocean at night. This would, the team hoped, limit the effects of solar heating and cooling on the helium, and altitude could be controlled without venting gas by adjusting the sand ballast. This balloon was christened *Double Eagle II*.

In St John's the British team had recovered from their

▲ *In the gondola (left to right): Max Anderson, Larry Newman and Ben Abruzzo.* Ben Abruzzo

fifth day of the flight, ninety-six hours out from Canada, the weather closed down. Heavy cumulo-nimbus clouds threatened *Zanussi*, and an extremely tired Cameron and Davey were forced down only 108 miles from the French coast. They waited in their gondola for a French trawler from a nearby fishing fleet to pick them up.

Two weeks later on 11 August, Anderson, Abruzzo and Newman took off from Presque Isle in *Double Eagle II*. The weather was favourable and the balloon flew steadily towards Europe after a shaky start when a down draught forced the balloon back onto the ground shortly after take-off. During the first two days there were also problems with communication — the radio in the gondola was faulty — but on the third day the problem was cleared. *Double Eagle II*'s track took them further north and higher than *Zanussi*, giving them problems with icing, and they ejected 3,250 pounds of ballast during the flight in order to maintain height. On the evening of the 16th, just before crossing the Irish coast, the three men jettisoned all the extra water and food, the life raft, and even bulkheads and floor boards to maintain a safe height over the British Isles. They were hoping for a landing in France.

They crossed Britain the following day, and on the evening of 13 August, 1978, 3,108 miles from Maine, *Double Eagle II* landed in a wheatfield at Evreux, near Misery, in Normandy. The envelope and gondola were surrounded by locals who had come out in their hundreds to welcome the three pilots, the first to cross the Atlantic Ocean by balloon. The flight took 135 hours 5 minutes and 50 seconds, which is still the longest time aloft for a manned balloon.

The skies above the Atlantic were abandoned to aeroplanes until 1984, when Joe Kittinger lifted off from Caribou in Maine. He left on the evening of 14 September — alone. He was attempting the first solo balloon crossing of the Atlantic, flying the 101,480-cubic-foot helium balloon, *Rosie O'Grady's Flying Circus*, from the now traditional boat-shaped open gondola beneath. Using information from meteorologist Bob Rice in Maine, Kittinger flew *Rosie O'Grady* into a quickly moving high weather system, riding a 57-knot westerly wind at 10,000 feet. The system slowed to 53 knots later and then to 25.

He made it look easy. The only major problem occurred after eighteen hours when the petrol stove exploded, enveloping the stern of the gondola in flames. Kittinger managed to put the fire out with an extinguisher before it did any major damage. By a judicious use of ballast *Rosie O'Grady* maintained an altitude of around 10,000 feet almost all the way to the Bay of Biscay, with Kittinger breathing oxygen through a mouthpiece for about half the flight to combat fatigue rather than to help in breathing.

Rosie O'Grady crossed the French coast on 17 September, after only sixty hours of flying, and kept on going eastwards across the Gascoyne of southern France. Ris-

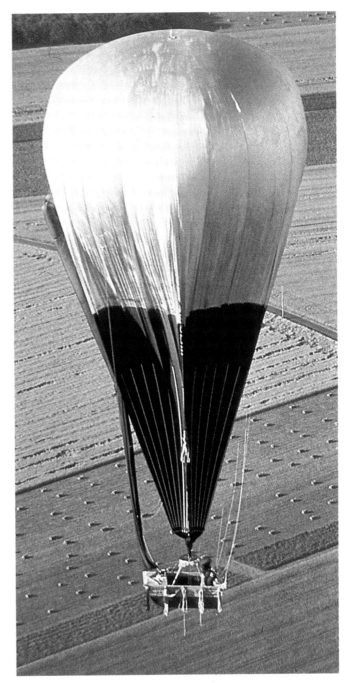

▲ Double Eagle II *prepared to land near Misery in Normandy, the historic crossing completed.* Ben Abruzzo

ing to 15,000 feet Kittinger flew over the Rhône estuary and across the Ligurian Sea at the border with Italy, where he reached the highest altitude of the flight at 17,200 feet. By this time most of the ballast had gone, and extra food, clothes and empty oxygen cylinders had all been jettisoned. Very tired after eighty-three hours of solo flying with just cat naps for sleep, Kittinger searched for a landing site in northern Italy. As he descended to 1,500 feet over the forest north of Savona, the surface wind began gusting to 25 knots in the vanguard of an approaching storm.

▲ *Over the Franco-Italian border after 80 hours and* Rosie O'Grady *reaches her greatest altitude of 17,200 feet. Kittinger starts to search for a landing site.* Joe Kittinger/National Geographic Society

◄ *The weather favoured an evening launch from Caribou on 14 September 1984, at 2020 hours local time.* Joseph Stancampiano/ National Geographic Society

▼ *After 60 hours flying,* Rosie O'Grady *is 12,000 feet above the Bay of Biscay, and Joe Kittinger takes a break before entering European airspace.* Joe Kittinger/National Geographic Society

▲ *Hélène Dorigny and Michel Arnould immediately before their record hot air duration flight.* Eric Sander (courtesy Hélène Dorigny and Gamma)

'Thunderstorms ahead and forests below,' Kittinger said. 'As a veteran balloonist I chose the latter.' *Rosie O'Grady* landed heavily on a wooded hillside at Cairo Montenotte. Kittinger was hurled ten feet out of the gondola by the 20-knot impact, and broke a bone in his right foot. This was almost as much of a shock to him as was his sudden arrival out of the sky to a party of woodcutters quietly going about their business. *Rosie O'Grady* had flown 3,543 miles in just 86 hours and 40 minutes — and Kittinger had completed the first solo crossing of the Atlantic and flown the greatest distance of any solo balloon flight. Italy welcomed him with Latin enthusiasm; he was given an audience with both the President and the Prime Minister as well as with Archbishop Foley of the Holy See.

Two years later, in the summer of 1986, Henk Brink of the Netherlands took off from St John's in Newfoundland in a combined helium/hot air balloon similar to the earlier *Zanussi*. Brink made a successful crossing of the Atlantic and, in a little-publicised flight, reached Holland near Ijmuiden and landed safely. He had flown a distance of 2,100 miles, one of the shortest and fastest crossings of the Pond. As yet, though, no hot air balloon had attempted a crossing. After *Double Eagle II*'s success Max Anderson had said: 'Even the largest hot air balloon can only carry enough fuel for a few hours' flight. The attempt has to be made with a helium balloon.'

These were words to tempt the devil. In the summer of 1984 Michel Arnould and Hélène Dorigny of France took off in a hot air balloon from the village of La Mele-sur-Sarthe, 93 miles east of Paris. The two aeronauts left the ground on 6 July at about 0530 hours. They flew for the rest of that day, through the night, and continued into the following day, the 7th. A remarkable sequence of wind changes helped them stay aloft as the wind veered from the north, to the north-east, into the east and then from the south-east.

Arnould and Dorigny finally landed at 2200 hours on the second night, a total of 40 hours 12 minutes and 5 seconds aloft. They touched down only about 60 miles west of Paris, but they calculated that they had flown a total distance of close to 250 miles. This remains the longest ever flight time for a hot air balloon. Michel Arnould was killed later in a micro-light accident. An Atlantic crossing was within reach, and by 1985 investigations had started in Britain into the mechanics of such a hot air balloon crossing.

Per Lindstrand, of Thunder & Colt Balloons in Shropshire, had assembled a team to assess the problems, and they decided on a high-altitude attempt in the lower levels of the jet stream at around 27,000 feet. This would involve a pressurised capsule. Oxygen masks are feasible at this height, but the flight was expected to take about two days, and forty-eight hours is a long time to be breathing through a mask. An envelope large enough to produce enough lift and strong enough to fly in the 100-knot-plus winds would also have to be developed.

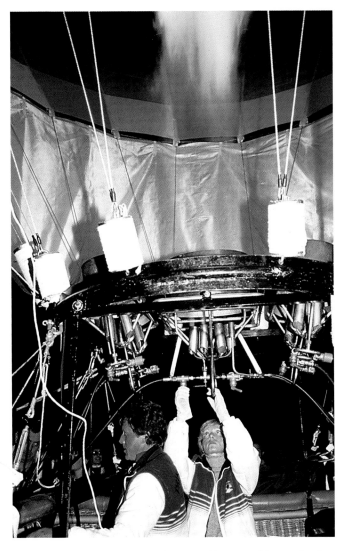

▲ *Just before take-off — and 40 hours 12 minutes and 5 seconds of flying.* Eric Sander (courtesy Hélène Dorigny and Gamma)

Further south, in the old port of Bristol, Don Cameron had decided to re-enter the Atlantic challenge. His team at Cameron Balloons opted for a flight path below the jet stream at between 10,000 and 15,000 feet above sea level, also using an enclosed capsule. Cameron commented: 'Many things could go wrong with both attempts.' It wasn't supposed to be a race, but with two of the largest balloon manufacturing companies in the world vying to build the first hot air balloon to cross the Atlantic, there was natural rivalry. Both take-offs were scheduled for mid-summer of 1987.

The high-altitude attempt used a capsule of aircraft aluminium coated with a protective layer of polystyrene. Six double cylinder fuel tanks, or pods, were fastened around the outside, the pressurising engine, heat exchanges and generators were fitted on top, and above them were positioned the eight burners to produce the necessary lift. The envelope was basically a single skin of nylon of 2.137 million cubic feet capacity standing 172 feet high. The lower half below the equator was a matt, black, heat-absorbent laminate on the outside, with a coating of aluminium-ised Melinex on the inside to prevent heat loss. Above the equator the envelope was coated with aluminiumised Melinex both inside and out, to reflect the radiated heat of the sun and to prevent heat loss as before. A second layer of fabric inside formed an insulating space, trapping heated air like a thermal suit. The theory was that, after inflation, the air temperature inside the envelope would be kept as stable as possible throughout the night and day.

It was the largest hot air balloon in the world, and at take-off weighed more than 10 tons. British adventurer Richard Branson brought his Virgin Airways into the attempt as the major sponsor, and the balloon was accordingly christened *Virgin Atlantic Flyer*. Branson would also fly as Lindstrand's co-pilot. *Virgin Flyer* was so high tech as to be almost incomparable to the first Montgolfière of 1783. Satellite Navigation, Omega, HF and VHF radios, micro-wave television links and reclining pilot chairs completed the advances of two hundred years of flying.

The lower altitude attempt was more traditional. The non-pressurised capsule would be 6 feet by 4 feet, also with a crew of two: Jim Howard would be Cameron's co-pilot. The envelope was an 850,000-cubic-foot design with enough lift to carry fifty people. 'Lindstrand and Branson will be able to fly higher,' said Cameron, 'but it could be a tortoise and hare race. I think our balloon is probably more reliable.'

The summer solstice of 1987 came and went with both

▲ *Per Lindstrand and Richard Branson about to board the capsule.* Thunder & Colt Balloons

teams waiting for the correct weather pattern — at St John's in Newfoundland and at Sugarloaf in Maine. Meteorologist Bob Rice then postponed the Lindstrand/Branson flight for almost a week because of bad weather. Cameron and Howard, 800 miles to the north, were also forced to postpone. Both teams were monitoring the other's progress and decisions but, unless one was affected by a local weather anomaly, the North Atlantic weather systems should have the same effect on each.

Then, on 2 July, the weather at Sugarloaf cleared overnight and in the early hours of the morning there was a weather 'window' through which *Virgin Flyer* could take off and climb to the jet stream. The conditions at St John's remained bad; no flying was possible. In the small hours of the morning under harsh arc lights *Virgin Flyer* was slowly inflated, a several-hour operation with 2 million cubic feet of envelope to fill. This was the first time the pilots had seen the envelope inflated.

At 0810 hours GMT (0410 local time) the largest hot air balloon in the world took off. A ballast line snagged one of the double fuel tanks and the pod was pulled off and fell to the ground. The now unbalanced balloon continued to rise quickly, and at 9,000 feet Lindstrand climbed out of the capsule to cut away some ballast to re-balance the balloon. After just over an hour *Virgin Atlantic Flyer* was cruising at 100 knots in the jet stream, the 'rivers in the sky'. At St John's Cameron and Howard remained earthbound. All they could do was wait and monitor the other balloon's progress.

Virgin Flyer flew eastwards uneventfully during the day until at 1813 GMT it had flown 914 miles, breaking the existing hot air distance record of 908 miles set by

◄ *Towards the end of the long burn to get enough lift for the ten-ton* Virgin Atlantic Flyer *to lift off.* Thunder & Colt Balloons

for three hours Lindstrand and Branson burned fuel hard to keep their height — within the black clouds there was no solar heating. At 2100 GMT they flew out of the front into the clear evening sunshine, on course and on schedule. The first of the double fuel tanks was now empty, and it was jettisoned under a drogue parachute into the ocean. With the pod lost during take-off there were now two pods gone, but three full ones remained.

Virgin Flyer crossed the half-way point, longitude 30 degrees west, just before dawn of the second day. 'Whatever that balloon had thrown at us then, whatever malfunctions had occurred, however much fuel we started to use, we were going to scrape home,' Lindstrand said afterwards.

During that second day, 3 July, very little fuel was burnt because of the heating effect of the sun. The problem was in fact the reverse — they had to keep venting hot air to stop climbing, almost losing control of the balloon about 400 miles from Ireland. *Virgin Flyer* was still travelling at an amazing 95 to 100 knots, and the Irish coast was quickly approaching. At 1330 GMT they crossed the coast above County Donegal, only twenty-nine hours after leaving the North American coast. The unexpected speed of the crossing presented new difficulties; three full pods of fuel remained slung

▲ *And she's away! Next stop, Europe. Note the fuel pods slung around the capsule.* Thunder & Colt Balloons

◄ Inset: *Over the North Atlantic the* Virgin Atlantic Flyer *runs her easting down.* Thunder & Colt Balloons
◄ *The 172 foot-high balloon at the point of lift off dwarfs the double storey house behind.* Thunder & Colt Balloons

◄ *Per Lindstrand at the contol module in the capsule. The escape hatch is above his head.* Thunder & Colt Balloons

Canadian Harold Warner in January 1985. The navigation system on board recorded the speed over the ground as 133 knots, which was taken for the new unofficial speed record. *Virgin Flyer* was flying on the front edge of a polar jet stream, but ahead were cold fronts with cumulo-nimbus clouds reaching as high as 45,000 feet. From the ground at Sugarloaf Rice advised Lindstrand and Branson to remain at 27,000 feet and fly through the frontal system. Lindstrand had a quick look down at 22,000 feet and then returned to 27,000 feet and flew into the front.

It was dark, it was snowing, the envelope and capsule shook and jerked in the turbulent, freezing cold air, and

on the outside of the capsule.

The surface weather in Scotland was bad, not good for landing at all, and so it was decided to land in Ireland after jettisoning the fuel pods over open country. There was a fuel tank especially for landing fitted inside the capsule.

They brought *Virgin Flyer* down through thick cloud from 27,000 feet to 2,000 feet before breaking into clear air. Londonderry aerodrome was sighted, while ahead lay Limavady, an area of farms and open fields a few miles inland from the Causeway Coast. Down came *Virgin Flyer*. The ground wind speed was 15 knots: the envelope was 2.3 million cubic feet.

The silver and black canopy with the white gondola beneath swooped over a farmyard. 'We saw the farmer and his wife looking up at us in amazement,' recalls Branson. 'We touched down with one hell of a bump, bounced five times, released the fuel tanks, then shot up with incredible speed.' The time was 1551 GMT, 31 hours and 41 minutes after take-off from Maine. *Virgin Flyer* had travelled 2,672 nautical miles, the greatest distance ever flown by a hot air balloon.

'I levelled the balloon out six feet below ground level,' a rueful Lindstrand admitted. 'The capsule was quite badly damaged,' said Branson. 'All our radios broke when we hit the ground.' They fought to regain control of the balloon. 'We had made contact, we had crossed the Atlantic,' Lindstrand explained, 'and so I decided the best thing to do would be to get safely down as soon as possible. The beaches around Benbane Head looked ideal.'

The speed of their trajectory took them past the beach and into the cold waters of the Irish Sea, splashing down about half a mile off-shore. Lindstrand reached forward and pushed the buttons to fire the bolts and release the giant envelope from the capsule. Nothing happened. They'd been tested three times in America.

He pressed again, but the explosive bolts wouldn't fire. The emergency battery system had shorted during the Limavady touch-down and there was no power — no power for the bolts and no power for the radios. They were isolated. The capsule was being dragged through the sea by the 2-million-cubic-foot envelope at about 15 knots as Lindstrand and Branson clambered out onto the top under the burners. There was a danger that the capsule could be dragged under if it acted like a submersible, one possibility that hadn't been tested. It was decided to evacuate.

'For God's sake, go!' Lindstrand said, and bailed out into the sea. *Virgin Flyer* actually began to rise as Branson hesitated and, relieved of Lindstrand's weight, it quickly soared to 50 feet and it was too late for him to jump. In the water below Lindstrand released his parachute to act as a marker. *Virgin Flyer* continued to rise, and levelled out in cloud at 3,900 feet. Branson brought the balloon down again, trying all the while to send a message on the radio about Lindstrand alone in the sea.

Descending out of the low cloud Branson saw the Royal Navy frigate HMS *Argonaut* steaming southwards and ditched *Virgin Flyer* close by, dropping into the sea upwind of the capsule seconds before the splashdown.

▲ *Inflation of* Double Eagle V *at Nagushimo, November 1981 —*
the first balloon to attempt the Pacific. Ben Abruzzo
◄ *The third and final landing, in the Irish Sea close by* HMS
Argonaut. Thunder & Colt Balloons

TRANS-PACIFIC

Two-thirds of the Earth is covered by sea and the largest ocean of them all is the Pacific, twice as wide as the Atlantic. Australian pilots Charles Kingsford-Smith and Charles Ulm, with crew Harry Lyon and James Warner of America, were the first to complete an aerial crossing of the Pacific in 1928. The flyers were greeted by 300,000 people when they arrived in Sydney. Since then the Pacific has been crossed in many a fashion. Scientific research and meteorological high-altitude balloons cross regularly, but no manned balloon had attempted a crossing until November 1981.

Ben Abruzzo and Larry Newman, from the *Double Eagle II* Atlantic crossing, were going for the double. This first manned attempt to cross the Pacific was in *Double Eagle V*, a 400,000-cubic-foot helium balloon designed for cruising at about 26,000 feet. The translucent envelope was made of polyethylene, barely 4½ millionths of an inch thick, and stood thirteen storeys high when inflated. The gondola was not pressurised. It was made of fibre-glass with a foam insulation, and measured 17 feet long, 7 feet high and 7 feet wide. Like the first such gondola of *The Small World*, it was also boat-shaped in case of ditching.

Flying with Abruzzo and Newman were Ron Clark and Rocky Aoki, and the total weight at take-off was a little more than 7 tons. Oxygen tanks to assist breathing at the higher altitudes were stored inside and outside the gondola, while ballast, in the form of sand, water and lead shot, accounted for more than half the total weight. 'The first law of ballooning,' Abruzzo stated, 'is that you stay aloft only as long as you have expendable ballast.'

The team assembled in late October, 1981, at Nagashima in Japan, on the east coast of Honshū. The weather systems looked promising for early November, and in the dark, small hours of the 10th at 0305 hours local time, *Double Eagle V* lifted off from Nagashima. The balloon climbed steadily upwards until at 12,348 feet it was level with the snow cap of Mount Fujiyama, now lying behind them. In the prevailing westerly winds *Double Eagle V* continued rising towards its 26,000-foot cruising altitude, but at 19,000 feet came the first hint of trouble.

Ice was accumulating and growing across the crown of the envelope, weighing the balloon down and distorting its thin fabric. They were 200 miles out over the Pacific, six hours into the crossing. The four men decided to descend again into warmer air to melt the ice. During the entire flight *Double Eagle V* was never able to ascend as planned into the 100 knot winds of the jet stream. The gondola was equipped to support the four men for ten days, but the deciding factor of the attempt would be the ballast.

A Sea King helicopter from *Argonaut* picked him up within minutes, and Lindstrand's position was then known. He in turn was picked up by a small boat as he was swimming to the shore, and then transferred by another Sea King. Neither man was injured; both were wet and cold.

So the Atlantic Ocean had at last been crossed by a hot air balloon, although the landing was a touch hairy, more like a moon-shot splashdown than a balloonist's drop into a vineyard. But then, there aren't many vineyards in Ireland. On the other side of the ocean Don Cameron and Jim Howard were still waiting in St John's for the weather to clear. To them the last word.

'Balloon pilots learn early on in their careers to accept what the climate throws at them; they come to terms with the fact that they might not be able to fly on a particular day. But to wait through half of June, and the whole of July and August, for zonal flow while someone else has it 800 miles further south was, to put it mildly, annoying.'

▲ *Operating the radio in the gondola, a thousand miles from anywhere.* Ben Abruzzo
◀ Double Eagle V *leaves Mount Fuji behind as she flies eastwards.* Ben Abruzzo
◀Inset: *Ice begins to coat the gondola, threatening to bring the balloon down into the sea.* Ben Abruzzo

As with all helium balloons, the gas contracted during the night and expanded during the day, and throughout the crossing the flight path of *Double Eagle V* went down and up accordingly. At about longitude 160 degrees east on 11 November it descended as low as 4,500 feet; later in the day at 175 degrees east it reached its maximum altitude of 22,000 feet. It was yo-yo ballooning. On 12 November at 0200 hours the balloon crossed the International Date Line at 17,500 feet, and the date on board was accordingly put back to the 11th again as they flew into longitudes west.

The calculations for jettisoning the diminishing ballast were now critical, and compromises had to be made between the desire for height and speed and the weight required to be ejected to achieve that. During the second 11 November and the morning of the 12th *Double Eagle V* flew a nearly level flight, which helped ease the ballast problem but at this height of between 15,000 and 16,000 feet the balloon's speed over the water was reduced to only 40 knots.

Double Eagle V was now east of Hawaii's longitude and at noon on the 12th, the fourth day of the attempt, the ambient air temperature dropped to such an extent that severe icing across the envelope threatened to bring the balloon down into the sea. Abruzzo estimated that the ice sheet over the crown weighed about 6,000 pounds, squashing the envelope beneath. In only two hours *Double Eagle V* was forced down 12,000 feet to a new low of 4,200 feet above the ocean, while all the crew could do was jettison 850 pounds of precious ballast. It seemed they were due for a ditching. Finally the warmer air nearer the sea began to melt the sheet of ice and it

began to break up, sending chunks of ice raining down onto the gondola. The envelope regained its shape and its lift, and the balloon rose again to 13,000 feet — this time into snow. Neither the fabric of the envelope nor the gondola was damaged, and snow was easily dealt with after the trauma of the ice.

The coast of California was now just 500 miles away, and although their ballast was down to only 1,500 pounds, the four began to believe they would make it. At 2100 hours local time on 12 November they passed over Point Arena, 6,900 feet below, and heard the breakers pounding the shore. For the first time *Double Eagle V* was flying over land.

They brought the balloon down through the clouds and found themselves flying in torrential rain. Only a few pounds of ballast remained, and with darkness upon them it was decided to land. Sanhedrin Mountain at 6,175 feet was ahead and slightly to the south when *Double Eagle V* descended in the darkness and rain near the town of Covelo. The approach was good and, as the balloon skimmed down, Abruzzo fired the explosive bolts to release the envelope; the gondola landed with a jolt on a bushy hillside at 2236 hours. The envelope came to rest further up the hillside before a stand of coniferous trees. No-one was injured — and they had crossed the Pacific.

Double Eagle V was the first and, so far, only manned balloon to fly from Asia to North America. It took 3 days, 12 hours and 31 minutes to make the crossing at an average speed of 68.3 miles per hour. Abruzzo, Newman, Clark and Aoki had flown 5,768 miles, a new distance record for any manned balloon and one that still stands today. Ben Abruzzo has since been killed in a light aeroplane crash which, with Max Anderson killed in Germany, leaves Larry Newman as the sole survivor of the *Double Eagle II* crew. Two hundred years have passed and flying is still a dangerous occupation.

▲ *Rocky Aoki presents his* cordon bleu *cooking —* Concorde *was never like this!* Ben Abruzzo

HIGHS AND LOWS

The perils of high-altitude flying became apparent as long ago as 1862 in the skies above Wolverhampton in Staffordshire. Physicist James Glaisher of the Royal Greenwich Observatory joined pioneer balloonist Henry Coxwell for an ascent on 5 September in *Mammoth*. On the ground the weather was misty, but at 7,000 feet they were clear of the clouds and in brilliant sunshine, rising rapidly. They released carrier pigeons at 15,700, at 21,000 and at 26,000 feet, which 'dropped like falling leaves' in the rarified air. At 29,000 feet the remaining birds began to die one by one through lack of oxygen, though Glaisher and Coxwell still felt no ill effects. By about 33,000 feet, however, both men were drowsy, their arms were numb, and their eyesight began to fail. Glaisher found he couldn't speak and then lost consciousness. They were suffering from severe hypoxia — oxygen starvation. Coxwell somehow managed to climb to the basket ring and pull the envelope valve with his teeth, and the hydrogen balloon began its 6-mile descent back to Staffordshire.

In 1875 in a French ascent, Messieurs Sivel and Croce-Spirelli died when their oxygen breathing equipment malfunctioned at 26,000 feet. Their pilot, the famous Gaston Tissander, also lost consciousness but survived to land the balloon safely. At the turn of the century Arthur Berson and Rheinard Süring of Germany at last broke Glaisher and Coxwell's record with an ascent to 35,433 feet in the hydrogen balloon *Prussia*. They were still riding in an open wicker basket but breathed oxygen through mouthpieces. This altitude record remained until 1927 when Captain Hawthorne Grey of the United States Army made the first stratospheric flight to 42,470 feet. He was forced to bail out of his hydrogen balloon during its descent and free fell and parachuted back to Earth. On his second attempt he stayed in the gondola and ascended to over 40,000 feet again, but for Grey it was a posthumous record. When the balloon landed he was found dead of hypoxia.

Four years later the bespectacled Professor Auguste Piccard and Paul Kipfer of Switzerland ascended to and returned safely from the stratosphere. They lifted off from Augsberg in Germany on 27 May 1931, and rose to

▼ *The* Mammoth, *in which James Glaisher and Henry Coxwell brushed with death in 1862, shown here over the Crystal Palace.* Royal Aeronautical Society

51,793 feet in a spherical, pressurised aluminium gondola suspended beneath an elongated envelope of hydrogen. This flight lasted twenty-four hours and the two scientists landed on the Gugl glacier high in the Italian Alps. In August the following year Piccard flew again and reached 53,152 feet with Maximillian Costyn as his assistant.

The pace quickened. In 1933 Fordney and Settle of America reached 54,675 feet, only to be beaten by three Russians later in the year in a hydrogen balloon called *Stratostat USSR*, a design very similar to Piccard's. They reached 58,700 feet. In January 1934 the Russians went again in *Ossoaviakluim* and reached an amazing 72,178 feet, but it was to be another posthumous record. The capsule parted from the envelope during the descent, and the final radio message from the pilot was: 'Condition serious — situation hopeless.' The escape hatch had jammed and the crew perished in the wild plunge back to Earth. In November 1935, using a massive 3.7-million-cubic-foot helium balloon called *Explorer II*, American captains Albert Stevens and Orvil Anderson ascended to 72,395 feet — 14 miles high.

The invention of plastics in Britain led to the development of polyethylene by the German scientist Otto Winzen, and this 'fabric' was used to make extremely light balloon envelopes for high-altitude research flights after the war. However, the previous altitude record remained until 2 June 1957, when Captain Joe Kittinger of the US Air Force took *Manhigh I* to 96,000 feet. *Manhigh* used a polythene 168,000-cubic-foot helium envelope and a pressurised capsule only 3 feet in diameter and just 8 feet long. The 100,000-foot barrier was broken in August 1957 by the balloon's successor, *Manhigh II*, this time with Major David Simons inside the pressurised capsule. He ascended to 101,516 feet above sea level, but the flight lasted longer than planned when turbulence and storms kept the balloon aloft for 32 hours and 10 minutes. Simons survived, and this flight time still stands as the longest for a pressurised balloon capsule.

Kittinger pushed the record still further in 1960 with *Excelsior III* and an ascent to 102,800 feet in an open gondola, from which he promptly bailed out. His resultant 4 minute and 38 second free fall in a pressurised suit exceeded the speed of sound before his parachute opened at 17,500 feet and brought him safely to ground. Although the envelopes of these balloons were large, the largest manned balloon ever flown was one of the *Strato-lab* series in 1961. On 4 May Commander Malcolm Ross and Lieutenant-Commander Victor Prather ascended to a dizzy 113,740 feet beneath a 12-million-cubic-foot helium envelope. They splashed down safely in the Gulf of Mexico after a fast descent, but Prather drowned while being picked up by a helicopter. The

▲ *The current hot air altitude record holder,* Stratoquest, *with pilot Per Lindstrand in the capsule, with all systems ready for launch.* Thunder & Colt Balloons

largest balloon of any type to date is one of 70 million cubic feet, a Winzen unmanned scientific balloon that stood as high as the Eiffel Tower.

Hot air balloons experience different problems from those of their gas cousins in high-altitude flying; envelope temperature, fuel supplies, and heater/burner problems in the rarefied and cold air are some. Julian Nott of Britain has almost taken a mortgage on the absolute hot air altitude record since 1972, when he first took it with an ascent to 35,959 feet using a carbon fibre and Kevlar gondola. He increased this altitude to 45,830 feet in 1974 with a flight over India in *Daffodil 2*, in which a pressurised capsule was used for the first time beneath a hot air envelope. In 1979 Chauncey Dunn of America took the record to 52,998 feet, and later that same year increased it further with a 53,198-foot ascent.

Nott immediately responded to the challenge and, in the following year, regained the record. He reached an altitude of 55,136 feet, experimenting with another pressurised capsule. As a break in 1984, Nott transferred to super-pressure balloons. He took one to 17,767 feet on 21 November, during a flight which also took the distance and duration records for super-pressure balloons to 1,486 miles and 33 hours 8 minutes and 42 seconds respectively.

Nott's hot air record understandably stood for eight years until, in the mid-summer of 1988, Per Lindstrand lifted off in the specially designed 600,000-cubic-foot *Stratoquest*. This balloon incorporated an ultra-light envelope of metalised fabric, developed by ICI in Britain, which could withstand temperature differences of 200 degrees Celsius inside to −70 degrees outside. The launch took place in ideal conditions from a paddock near the old cowboy town of Laredo, in Texas, on 6 June at 0543 hours. The now standard capsule was pressurised at 25,000 feet, and *Stratoquest* rose at between 1,000 and 1,500 feet per minute. Ice formed on the outside of the capsule as it passed through the stratosphere, then Nott's 55,136-foot mark was passed; Lindstrand stopped the ascent at 64,997 feet. The descent was begun, but the solar heating effect was greater than expected and Lindstrand had to vent when the rate decreased to only

▲ *In the darkness of the early morning the large envelope is inflated.* Thunder & Colt Balloons

◄ *Jean-Robert Cornuel sets forth in search of Orpheus, a quarter of a mile below the surface.* Jean-Robert Cornuel

▼ *The 600,000-cubic-foot* Stratoquest, *in the final stages of its descent above Texas, having set the new record.* Thunder & Colt Balloons

▲ Canson *is towed across a modern Styx, a subterranean lake deep in the Bournillon Caves.* Jean-Robert Cornuel

and echoed in the cave the balloon rose slowly from the floor, casting weird and fantastic shadows over the uneven walls.

For this ascent the pilot had to be directed from outside the basket, in order to prevent the crown of the envelope from catching the jagged roof of the cave; for once the pilot needed to see directly above him. There was also no wind below ground, so *Canson* had to be towed by hand. Jean-Robert flew over a lake and down to the darkness at the bottom of the cave. Just the thought of carrying all the equipment back to the surface was tiring, so Jean-Robert flew *Canson* slowly upwards through the ancient underground system of caves and lakes with a gentle hand on the burner throttle. To show that depth flying wasn't a fluke Jean-Robert repeated the flight in January 1988 for Japanese television.

Monsieur Cornuel doesn't fly underground all the time; he is one of the few to have flown in a hot air balloon over Mont Blanc in the French Alps, a quite respectable height of 15,770 feet. Yet for the ultimate in mountain flying one must surely follow the mountaineers, out of Europe to Nepal, and it is to there we travel for the last of the record breakers.

400 feet per minute. *Stratoquest* landed safely in a dry grass field 70 miles from the launching site at 0911 hours, with a new altitude record.

So much for height, what about depth? There aren't any official records recognised by the Féderation Aéronautique Internationale but, if there were, Jean-Robert Cornuel of France might claim the lowest hot air balloon flight — 1,312 feet below ground level. This rare flight took place on 28 August 1987 at Vercors in the Bournillon Caves.

Jean-Robert and his crew carried the *Canson* balloon down through a series of massive limestone caves a distance of nearly 2,000 feet, and into a 100-foot-high chamber. The floor of the cave was strewn with boulders and rockfalls from the roof, so the envelope was laid out over a carpet to protect it from snags and tears. Under artificial light in the cold, dank cave inflation began, using a 'developed/flat layer' technique whereby hot air was blown into the envelope from the beginning. 'It's not the classic way of inflation,' said Jean-Robert, 'but in this case very effective!' As the burners roared

ATTEMPT ON EVEREST

The Himalayas are the highest mountain ranges in the world and also the youngest. They were formed when the Indian sub-continent moved northwards and collided with the massive Asian continental plate. India is still moving northward at a rate of about 2 inches per year, and the Himalayas are still being formed, are still getting higher.

Mount Everest — Qomolangma or Sagamatha, 'the dwelling place of the gods' — was first climbed by a British expedition; Sir Edmund Hillary of New Zealand and Tensing Norgay Sherpa of Nepal reached the summit on 29 May 1953. Since then the highest peak in the world has been climbed in almost every possible way, from all sides, with and without oxygen. It's even been skied down. But Everest has never been flown over by balloon, and in November 1985 an Australian team led by Chris Dewhirst arrived in Kathmandu to try their hand.

Everest is more than 29,000 feet above sea level and more than 5 miles high, and oxygen-assisted breathing was necessary in the open baskets. The winds, of course, would decide the final status of the attempt; the balloon might pass alongside the mountain, skirt the summit, or actually fly over the top. If this last did happen the landing would almost certainly be in Chinese-controlled Tibet, and therein was another area of political and immigration problems.

The attempt used two hot air balloons named after the expedition's major sponsors. With Dewhirst in *J&B* were Aden Wickes, a Qantas pilot, and British adventurer and film-maker Leo Dickinson. In *Zanussi* were Australian balloon manufacturers Phil Kavanagh and Brian Smith, and photo-journalist Jan Reynolds from America. Martin Harris of Britain was the meteorologist, and a supporting team of a further eighteen people included ground crew, cameramen and supporters. The two 203,000-cubic-foot envelopes were especially designed and manufactured by Phil Kavanagh, and he also made a smaller version of each for acclimatisation and filming flights.

The expedition began on 28 August 1985, when an old Bedford lorry with 3 tons of equipment was swung aboard the Indian freighter *Chandidas* alongside the Melbourne docks. A month later it landed on the wharf in Calcutta. A further 1,000 miles across the Ganges flood plain and northwards along the old trunk roads of the British Raj and the lorry reached the rendezvous at

◄ Facing page: *High altitude free-fall parachute training over New South Wales. Going . . . going . . . gone.* Chris Dewhirst
◄ Inset: *Preparation and training in Australia. Phil Kavanagh manufacturing the 203,000-cubic-foot balloons in his Sydney workshop.* Chris Dewhirst
▼ *A Montgolfière takes off amidst the temples of ancient Bhaktapur.* Chris Dewhirst

135

Kathmandu, the traditional staging post for Everest expeditions. The other members flew into Kathmandu from Australia, Britain and America, and the expedition was ready to go.

Rain, hail, snow and high winds greeted them in Nepal as storms raged about the mountains. Massive landslides destroyed bridges, while villages were devastated and crops ruined. In the Kathmandu Valley the expedition made two flights using the smaller test envelopes. In the ancient city of Bhaktapur, the old seat of the Nepalese kings, *J&B* and *Zanussi* were inflated in Dubar Square, a small clearing squeezed between four Hindu temples some 1,500 years old. A temple keeper, armed with a wicked-looking sword, was one of hundreds of locals who crowded the square, eagerly helping with the launches. The launch day was also a festival day, and the crowd was perhaps the largest ground crew in the history of ballooning.

Chris Dewhirst had a worrying vision: 'I was standing amongst the ruins of the most priceless and ancient temple in Nepal; they were as fragile as a house of cards, and a collision with a temple would have been the end of it all.'

The two balloons lifted above the delicate temples while the Nepalese flowed like a river along the muddy paths and lanes below, following this modern miracle of lighter-than-air flight. Jets, turbo-props and choppers were *passé* in Nepal, but these new-fangled balloons! So as not to offend the other gods, the balloons were then taken to the Buddhist temple at Bhodnath for more flights.

The plan was to take off for Everest from Kathmandu but to acclimatise for this high-altitude flight in a series of moves to camps at progressively higher altitudes. The first camp was at Khunde, 12,000 feet above sea level.

◄ *The new passes by the old.* Chris Dewhirst
► *After the storms much of the travelling in the foothills was restricted to just that — foot work.* Phil Kavanagh
▼ *During the move to the higher regions for acclimatisation, four feet were often needed.* Mike Dillon (courtesy Chris Dewhirst)

Still using the smaller envelopes, the two balloons made the first ever Himalayan hot air flights, one hour over the Khunde plateau, ascending to 15,000 feet above sea level. After acclimatisation the expedition made its second move, higher again to Thayangboche below the south face of Everest, a traditional passing-through point for mountaineering expeditions. Fully acclimatised the teams returned to Kathmandu.

It was here that meteorologist Martin Harris came into his own, gathering video and analogue information from the NOAA satellite system with his special equipment. The two crews obviously wanted to fly as soon as possible before their altitude acclimatisation wore away; the pressure on Harris was great. It wasn't eased by recurrent bouts of amoebic dysentery, though no-one's bowels were in top working order by this time: that was an accepted part of an Everest attempt.

To fly over 'the roof of the world' the balloons would attempt to use the 60-knot winds of the jet stream above 25,000 feet, and the bitter air temperature of about −40 degrees Celsius, standard November conditions. These conditions would blow the balloons fast enough and allow an envelope temperature low enough — about 80 degrees Celsius — to provide enough lift to cross Everest. The flight would take about three hours, but double the required amount of fuel was carried. The crews sat and waited for the correct weather patterns.

After six days the forecast was good. A satellite pass gave a favourable prognosis for the following morning: the decision was taken to go. The baskets and gear were already laid out on the launching field, and at 0400 hours on the 10th inflation of the large envelopes began.

Then Harris arrived with an amended forecast; low-altitude cloud was forming over the mountains. This would have no effect on the high-altitude flight but would certainly affect landing and make navigation difficult by obscuring the valleys and ridges. An immediate conference took place, an anxious and tense meeting in the cold dawn of Kathmandu Valley.

'This was a crucial discussion,' Dewhirst said, 'and even in retrospect we made the right decision.' The momentum from the years of preparation and the atmosphere of the moment carried the day; only a change in the high altitude weather would have halted the launch.

▲ Zanussi, *using the smaller training envelope, on the Khunde Plateau.* Mandy Dickinson (courtesy Chris Dewhirst)
▶ *The attempt on Everest begins, and the two balloons fly towards the 'roof of the world'.* Leo Dickinson (courtesy Chris Dewhirst)
▼ *A less than ideal inflation of* J & B *in the morning mist of Nepal.* Leo Dickinson (courtesy Chris Dewhirst)

Inflation was completed and the two balloons stood upright, swaying in the early November mist. Lift-off was scheduled for 0615. *Zanussi* climbed ahead of and above *J&B* towards the low cloud ceiling of 450 feet. Suddenly, at 300 feet, a powerful wind shear struck *Zanussi* with Kavanagh, Smith and Reynolds, twisting it through 180 degrees and slamming the basket into the envelope of *J&B* beneath. The lower canopy caved in, and in their basket Dewhirst, Wickes and Dickinson waited for the worst, for the thin nylon to tear apart and send them plummeting back to the ground. There was nothing they could do; to burn or vent would only have increased the danger and the damage to the fabric. Above them Kavanagh leaned perilously out of his basket fending off the envelope while Smith fired on all burners to get maximum lift. *Zanussi's* basket rolled off *J&B* and soared away, climbing rapidly into the grey clouds. *J&B* followed, undamaged, and the shouting upturned faces on the ground below disappeared.

At 1,000 feet above the ground the two balloons broke through the dull clouds into glorious crisp sunshine. Oxygen masks were donned. *J&B* was now slightly higher and about 1,000 yards ahead of *Zanussi* and, burning steadily, rose to 20,250 feet to clear the peak of Nambur. *Zanussi* levelled out at 15,500 feet: one of the oxygen leads had come loose, Smith advised over the radio, but after some adjustments they continued their climb upwards.

The loose lead was the only equipment problem, but after half an hour Dewhirst calculated that they were burning fuel at more than double the planned rate — one cylinder was already empty — and the temperature in the open basket was unexpectedly mild. Something was wrong. Kavanagh and Smith confirmed the same situation in *Zanussi*, and said they were perspiring heavily in their protective polar clothing. At 23,000 feet

the atmospheric temperature was steady, but only at freezing point instead of the forecast -40 degrees; much more fuel would have to be burnt to achieve the necessary lift. This was a serious blow to the attempt on Everest.

The balloons were on course for the mountain, but here there was another problem. Instead of the expected 60-knot wind it was only about 30 knots. 'Here we were,' said Dewhirst, 'in typically calm summer weather yet high above the Himalayas on the verge of winter. We had a problem.' Despite carrying double the amount

of fuel needed for the flight, a quick calculation showed that they would now be short by about 25 per cent to reach Everest. The three-year dream of taking the first balloons to Everest had disappeared in the first half-hour of the flight.

But ballooning is like that, the weather controls all. Yet the alpine height record could still be broken; balloonists had at least learnt to be adaptable. With Wickes flying, Dewhirst navigating, and Dickinson filming, *J&B* was gradually taken above 25,500 feet while *Zanussi* monitored from below at 24,000 feet. At 25,750 feet the

record was broken. After two hours' flying they had won a consolation prize for missing Everest, and it was all on film. When *J&B* descended to *Zanussi*'s altitude the two balloons were only 15 miles short of Everest but with 85 per cent of their fuel used, and it was agreed to begin the descent.

J&B began to lose altitude. All at once, all three pilot lights went out; the increase of oxygen in the air had caused a surge that Dewhirst and Wickes missed, and the surge blew all the pilots out. In the rarefied air with no burners the balloon began to lose height alarmingly,

▲ *At 25,750 feet above sea level a new mountain altitude record is claimed.* Inset: *As Everest comes closer and the balloons gain more height oxygen masks are donned to eliminate any possibility of hypoxia.* Leo Dickinson (courtesy Chris Dewhirst)

out of control. Kavanagh and Smith watched from a thousand yards away, wondering why the radio had gone suddenly silent.

'Are they falling or are we rising?' asked Reynolds. 'They're in trouble,' replied Kavanagh. *Zanussi* followed them down, under control.

Striking match after match, Dewhirst and Wickes desperately tried to re-light the pilots, but the lack of oxygen and the speed of descent immediately snuffed each match out. A peizo spark ignitor is no good at more than 12,000 feet because of the rarefied air. *J&B* plummeted earthwards at more than 1,000 feet per minute, the envelope still full, but full of useless, cold air. Through the bottom of the basket, despite the canvas covering, freezing air blasted upwards onto the crew, chilling them to the bone. Dickinson kept filming, but as the altimeter sped past 18,000 feet — only a couple of thousand feet above the mountains — he swung one leg out over the side of the basket with his spare hand on the ripcord of his parachute. Wickes started the countdown for bailing out.

Dewhirst at last managed to re-light one of the pilots and a burner roared again. Then the other pilots flared and all the burners were roaring. Control of *J&B* was regained, at less than 900 feet above the ice ridges of the Panch Pokhari valley. Dickinson climbed back into the basket, still filming.

At 14,600 feet above sea level *J&B* descended into a valley, out of the jet stream. The low cloud cover had cleared and *Zanussi*, farther behind because of *J&B*'s rapid descent, followed. A northerly air current over the rhododendron tree line swung *J&B* along the valley towards its western ridge, and all eyes were searching for a landing site. Protective helmets were donned. Three hundred yards ahead they saw a flat plateau of

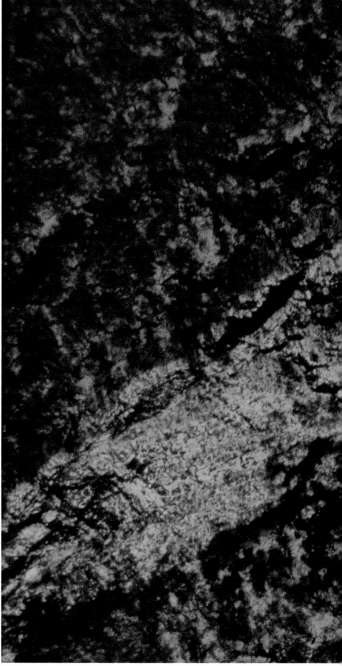

▲ *With all burner lights extinguished,* J & B *plummets at more than 1,000 feet per minute towards Panch Pokhari valley.* Phil Kavanagh
◄ *The retrieve helicopter picks up the two crews after a night's camping in the Himalaya.* Leo Dickinson (courtesy Chris Dewhirst)

ice, clear of rhododendrons and offering a good chance to save the envelope. *Zanussi* swooped over them, caught in an upward current, and disappeared over the ridge.

Wickes put *J&B*'s basket down into bushes and Dewhirst leapt out with a tether rope while Wickes intermittently burned again. They dragged and cajoled the 203,000-cubic-metre balloon across to the snow and

down to the ice plateau — ten minutes of exhausting, frantic physical effort that left Dewhirst seeing stars; at 12,000 feet above sea level the air contains 50 per cent less oxygen. The envelope was saved.

Meanwhile, Smith and Kavanagh were battling to save *Zanussi* in the next valley, riding thermals and cross-currents above the warmer, east-facing ridge. After a turmoil of twisting and spinning they were finally left with a choice between colliding with a jagged rock face or venting rapidly and dropping into large rhododendron trees. They chose the safer option, and *Zanussi* touched down into the foliage, the branches cracking and breaking apart beneath the basket as the envelope 'gift wrapped' the trees above.

The crews spent the night with their balloons, and in the morning laid out over the snow the green and yellow *J&B* envelope as a marker and radioed for the waiting helicopter. The nearest village was a day and a half's walk away, across impossible terrain, but the teams were determined not to leave any gear in the mountains. It took three days to air-lift it all out.

Dewhirst summed up the feelings of the expedition when they were all re-united on 14 November in Kathmandu. 'We were disappointed we hadn't reached Everest, but we'd still made the first balloon flight over the Himalayas. And we'd set a new record for the highest ever alpine flight, and no one had been hurt. We hadn't done too badly.'

TOWARDS 2000

*A*S THE last decade of the twentieth century begins, the ecology of the Earth has become one of the major international issues. 'Ozone depletion' and 'greenhouse effect' are now household words. Even ballooning has been touched, not least by the global changes of the weather, so it's fitting that balloons are now being used to investigate and highlight these urgent problems.

On 22 April 1989, the first ever balloon to fly at the North Pole lifted off from the slushy, unusually thin sea ice at 90 degrees north. The balloon was the 77,000-cubic-foot hot air *Rainbow Endeavour* of the private Norwegian/British group, Global Concern. It was suspected that the unseasonably warm Arctic spring that had melted so much ice at the Pole was caused by a combination of the hole in the ozone layer over the Arctic and the greenhouse effect, exactly what Global Concern had come to the region to publicise. *Rainbow Endeavour* and pilot Paul Lavelle had been brought north from Eureka in the North West Territories by a de Havilland Twin Otter, but because of the slushy ice even this ski-equipped aeroplane had had to land 6 miles away from the Pole. The balloon and equipment were hauled by sled across the moving ice to 90 degrees north, the exact geographical spot determined by satellite navigation.

The publicity flight was a combined British, Norwegian

and Canadian effort, and television and newspaper cameras were on hand to record the historic ascent. When next you go ballooning think about some of the items you take with you. Reject those halon fire extinguishers, CFC aerosol sprays, plastic 'blown foam' packaging and, if you are flying in cold conditions like the *Rainbow Endeavour*, foam insulation; they *all* attack and destroy the life-preserving ozone layer.

Environmental balloons are also being developed for the Antarctic. The proposal is to carry small generators into the atmosphere in an attempt to slow down the expansion of the hole in the ozone. A prototype is being tested by Thunder and Colt Balloons.

▲ *Landing on the sea ice after the historic flight, and presenting one of the more difficult retrieves of international ballooning.* Global Concern

◄ *Previous page: The Anglo-Russian glasnost balloon ghosting low over the River Vilija, the national flags in bright contrast to the dark green of the Baltic pines along the river banks.* Cameron Balloons

Glasnost and *perestroika* are also household words now, and ballooning is playing its part in promoting the growing friendship between the previously hostile nations engaged in the Cold War. The first ever international balloon meet to be held in Russia took place in 1989, from 26 to 29 May. Thirty hot air balloon teams from around the world, a total of 114 people, were invited to Vilnius, capital of the Baltic state of Lithuania, for a celebration of flying, fun and *glasnost*. This breakthrough festival is hopefully the first of an annual event, each meet to be held in a different city in Russia.

This historic event followed the agreement of September 1988 between Cameron Balloons of Britain, Lenin Komsomel, a Russian youth organisation, and Sotrudni-chestvo, a Moscow co-operative. During its first year of production this joint venture company intends to manufacture fifty balloons for Russian and East European countries. 'If you ask me how big the market for balloons is going to be in the Soviet Union, the honest answer is, I don't know,' said Don Cameron. 'Our partners represent a very powerful group of interests, both state and private, and they are certain the sport will become very popular very quickly.'

▲ *The* Rainbow Endeavour *flying over the geographical North Pole — latitude 90 degrees north, longitude 55 degrees 14 minutes west — on 22 April 1989.* Global Concern

▶ *Before 2000, perhaps Eastern Europe and Russia will witness a sight such as this.* Thom Roberts

A golden pagoda of Japan flies before the country's highest and sacred mountain, Fujiama. Alain Guillou/Leica

A 77,000-cubic-foot *glasnost* balloon from Camerons is already flying, with huge Russian and British flags around the envelope, and pilot training and promotion have begun. A balloon factory has been built 30 miles outside Moscow, and production began in the autumn of 1989. The Russian authorities have also invited Don Cameron to attempt a celebratory flight from Britain across Europe to Russia. Cameron has accepted the challenge, and will use a combined helium and hot air balloon to make the flight from Bristol to, hopefully, Leningrad. On the heels of the meet at Vilnius came a second in Russia, in July 1989. Again, balloonists from around the world were invited.

Cameron is also toying with the idea of a trans-Atlantic race sometime in the 1990s. He has plans for a field of up to ten balloons to take off from St John's in Newfoundland to race across the North Atlantic, the winner being the first to touch down east of a line of longitude in Europe. 'It's an unfulfilled dream,' he says. 'I'll worry about this race when we have a sponsor.'

As in almost every sport, sponsorship plays a vital part in paying for the various events, championships and expeditions, but some balloonists are fighting this. In November 1988, a meet was held at Marsh Benham, near Newbury in Royal Berkshire, for small Viva 65 balloons — with no sponsors of the event or of the balloons. Eleven hot air balloons flew, and a second meet was held in the Lake District in the north of England in 1989. There *is* life after sponsorship, however limited, but don't be surprised if you come across the occasional Moët-Chandon balloon during the next few years. This famous vintner celebrates its 250th anniversary in 1993, and its balloon is flying over the 250 most famous and spectacular sites around the world for a commemorative film.

The various balloon championships will continue, in particular the World Hot Air Championships held every odd year. The 1989 Worlds were held in Japan in November on Kyūshū Island at Saga, to coincide with the hundredth birthday of this castle town. Saga has

▲ *Fujisan (12,388 feet) was first crossed by balloon on 25 July 1976;* Cathay Pacific I, *with Geoff Green of Hong Kong, and* Ascension II, *with Sabu Ichiyoshi of Japan, flew from Fujinomiya City to Yamashi Prefecture. The flight took two hours.* Cathay Pacific

▲ *Touch . . . and go.* Thom Roberts

◄ *Japan's* Flying Baby, *by the Clifton Suspension Bridge, Bristol. For those who aren't fluent in Japanese, the writing on the nappy advertises paper tissues.* Cameron Balloons

become the ballooning capital of the country. The Saga prefecture is largely an agricultural area, ideal for ballooning in a country of little flat land, yet even so the rice fields are small and landing must always be precise. The coast and the intruding sea of Ariake-wan provide another hazard for the unwary pilot.

These ninth World Championships were the first to be held in Asia, for which much of the credit should go to Sabu Ichiyoshi of Tokyo. Canada will be host to the next Worlds in 1991, to be flown over the tranquil scenery of St Jean-sur-Richelieu in Quebec, while Belgium and India are vying for the 1993 championships. The remaining three venues before 2000 have not yet been chosen.

There are now championships for virtually every type of lighter-than-air flying machine — even hot air airships have a world championship. The first was held in Luxembourg in August 1988, and was won by Oscar

Lindstrom flying a Thunder & Colt AS-56. In the United States, after a run of eighteen years, the venue for its national championships has at last been changed. From Indianola in Iowa the meet was moved to Baton Rouge in Louisiana for the 1989 competition.

In September 1989 the enthusiastic Indian ballooning fraternity held a unique gathering beside the Taj Mahal in Agra. Balloonists from abroad were invited to fly over this monument to love, and it is hoped that India will stage more fiestas during the 1990s.

Africa is also becoming more and more popular with balloonists, and Brian Smith of Britain has organised the first international meeting in Zimbabwe. It is scheduled to take place at Harare in April 1990, and balloonists from many countries have been invited to the beautiful capital of the old Rhodesia.

The designers and manufacturers of the spectacular Special Shapes continue to surprise the world with bizarre larger-than-life replicas. As if a flying opera house and an inflatable Jumbo jet aren't difficult enough to fly and deflate, a flying cow is now on the drawing board. Advice is requested from dairy farmers as to the best way to deflate the udder.

Special Shape balloons have now been elevated to an art form, and almost anything seems possible. Austrian artist André Heller introduced a 'magical suspension of belief' to the skies over Europe in 1986 — his Flying Sculptures. The airborne shapes of his childhood fantasies caused such a stir during their eight-city tour of western Europe that Vienna sponsored a similar tour to North America the following year. The response was just as great when these imaginative Montgolfières flew over thirty more cities in that continent.

▲ *Poking a cheeky tongue at officialdom, Heller's* Children's Moon *flies over Washington during its North American tour of 1988.* David Partridge

▶ *The Thunder & Colt* Financial Times *at Tower Bridge, celebrating the centenary of that respected newspaper. It took hours to produce the 'copy' for the front page.* Thunder & Colt Balloons

◀ UFO *and* Kiku *float through the mists above the Niagara Falls.* David Partridge

These Flying Sculptures — *Kiku*, a gift of love to Heller's girlfriend, *Children's Moon*, complete with eyes and a tongue, and *UFO*, an airborne sea anemone — had made 156 million media contacts in Europe, and in North America in 1987 this was complemented by coverage in 530 newspapers alone. The sculptures were built by Thunder & Colt of Shropshire, and the tours organised by Air 2 Air of Bristol and the Hot Air Balloon Company of Fairoaks in Kent.

Creative art is difficult to fly, however, and pilots David Partridge, Tom Holt Wilson and Tom Donnelly of Britain drew up a list of the foibles of each aircraft. The large black *Kiku* flew very slowly in thermal heat, had very positive control, and could hold altitude for minutes without burning. But it was also a slow and laborious process to deflate, as there was no vent in the upper cone and only velcro slits in the appendages. *Children's Moon* was 'twitchy', with remarkable defor-

▲ *And pure futurism in America.* David Partridge

coming down in the sea. Yet this was a valid attempt, and for Japanese balloonists the Pacific crossing is as important as the Atlantic was for Americans.

The first attempt on the Pacific by a hot air balloon took place in November 1989 at Miyakonojo in north Japan. The team was built around the successful *Virgin Atlantic Flyer* attempt, with Per Lindstrand as chief pilot and Richard Branson as co-pilot. The gigantic *Virgin Pacific Flyer* balloon stood higher than Nelson's Column, had a capacity of 2.5 million cubic feet, and carried 6 tonnes of liquid propane. The flight plan would take *Pacific Flyer* into the easterly flowing jet stream with speeds of up to 200 knots expected.

After a part-inflation on the twentyfourth, a second attempt was made the following evening. Freezing ground conditions and wind delayed inflation until 2300 hours when, as the envelope expanded, it was found that the outer heat-retaining film had delaminated from the fabric because of the frost. When the balloon was fully inflated it was discovered that the inner film had also delaminated. The launch was aborted. A better launch site has since been found at Myakonojo, the envelope has been repaired, and another attempt will be made.

In Britain, Anthony Smith is running the increasingly popular invitation Long Jump every October. About thirty balloons now compete for as long a distance as possible in one flight. This is a surprisingly hard task because of the geographical limitations of the British Isles, and great skill and fortune are needed to make long flights; the current record distance for the Long Jump at 1989 is only 169 nautical miles. The longest ever balloon flight recorded within the United Kingdom took place on 30 October 30 1918 when the military balloon *W1* flew 210 miles, from the Hurlingham Club in London to Bickley Moor in Yorkshire. The hydrogen balloon ascended into a gale, and at times travelled at more than 60 knots over the ground in its helter-skelter journey northwards. During the flight, when the balloon began to lose height after venting and there was little ballast left, a Royal Navy officer in the crew offered to lighten the load; he also had a date that evening in London. *W1* was brought close to the ground and this member of the Senior Service bailed out into a field. He caught a train back to town while the balloon soared away to Yorkshire.

Airships, too, are staging a return. Goodyear of the United States is still flying four remaining from the 300 built this century, but the major promoter is now Airship Industries of Great Britain. Since 1980 this company has built sixteen, of which fourteen are currently flying; five in North America, four in Europe, two each in Australia and Japan, and one in Korea. They are used mainly for corporate advertising and joy flights, but

mations in gusts and cross winds. Because of the tail of the envelope, pilot visibility was reduced, and handling on the ground proved very difficult. The *UFO* was the most stable, and was accordingly inflated first, but in thermals and whilst descending its flat base made it skid through the air.

Records will no doubt continue to be broken in all areas of ballooning. No hot air balloon has crossed the English Channel from France to England, no balloon has completed a non-stop crossing of Australia, the Indian Ocean awaits a manned crossing in any direction, while both the Atlantic and the Pacific await an east-to-west flight. In early 1989 Fumio Niwa of Japan attempted a second crossing of the Pacific using a high-tech gas balloon, but didn't get very far. He took off on 14 February, but only managed 20 miles or so before

▲ *Japan's Fumio Niwa with the capsule of his 1989 trans-Pacific attempt.* Courtesy Sabu Ichiyoshi
◀ *14 February 1989, and Fumio Niwa lifts off for the Pacific Ocean.* Courtesy Sabu Ichiyoshi
▼ *One of the famous Goodyear helium airships at Sardinia in 1984 during the world twelve-metre sailing championships.* Sally Samins

days without refuelling. It will carry sophisticated radar and detection equipment for coastal surveillance of other aircraft, submarines, mines and various missiles, and incorporates vectored thrust engines. The propellers of these engines can be turned to any angle at all, enabling the aircraft to fly forwards, backwards, upwards and downwards, and even to hover if necessary. The *YEZ-2A* is a lighter-than-air combination of the

◄ *A more recent Cameron hot air airship over the Alps.* Cameron Balloons
► *Manufacturer's model of the* Sentinel 5000/YEZ-2A *airship.* Airship Industries
▼ *Pedal power and helium mixture; developments sometimes seem to go backwards.* Balloon Aloft

they have more serious uses, too. In Australia, for example, the Commonwealth Scientific and Industrial Research Organisation is using airships for geological surveys of remote areas of the outback, and is now extending this to include surveys of the Pacific Ocean. In the northern hemisphere airships are also used in the search for and control of marine pollution.

The revolution in modern airships is typified by the Sentinel 5000 concept for the United States Department of Defence. Designed by Roger Monk, technical director and founder of Airship Industries, this helium airship, designated the *YEZ-2A* by the US Navy, is 425 feet long, has a capacity of 2.5 million cubic feet, a pressurised gondola of three decks, and a flying capability of five

Hawker jump jet and a helicopter.

A British-American consortium has been established to develop the new aircraft — Westinghouse-Airship Industries Incorporated — and is supported by a $US170 million contract. 'Fly-by-wire' control is a recent innovation for commercial and fighter aeroplanes, but *YEZ-2A* is the first to utilise 'fly-by-light' control, developed in conjunction with GEC Avionics. Commands to the rudder and elevators of the blimp are sent by coded light beams from a digital computer along fibre-optic cables: all the pilot on the flight deck has to do is waggle a small joy stick rather like a computer game control. The building of the first operational development model began in early 1990.

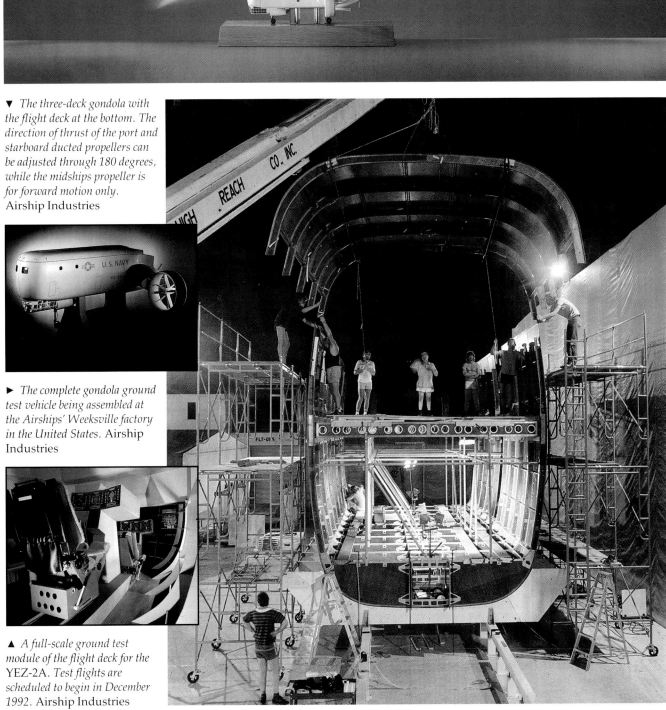

▼ *The three-deck gondola with the flight deck at the bottom. The direction of thrust of the port and starboard ducted propellers can be adjusted through 180 degrees, while the midships propeller is for forward motion only.* Airship Industries

► *The complete gondola ground test vehicle being assembled at the Airships' Weeksville factory in the United States.* Airship Industries

▲ *A full-scale ground test module of the flight deck for the YEZ-2A. Test flights are scheduled to begin in December 1992.* Airship Industries

EXPEDITIONS

Various expeditions are being planned around the world for the 1990s. One of the first is in South America with the core members from the team that attempted Everest in 1985. Led by Chris Dewhirst, the team includes Phil Kavanagh, Brian Smith, Peter Counsell, Leo Dickinson and Jan Reynolds.

Dewhirst intends to fly two hot air balloons from the plain of Nazca, 250 miles south of Lima. The balloons will climb to between 20,000 and 30,000 feet and use the prevailing 30-knot westerly winds to cross the high central ridge of the Andes, the Cordillera. Once over this range the two balloons will attempt to land at or close by Machu Picchu, the 'lost' city of the Incas on the eastern slopes of the Andes. Machu Picchu is 12,000 feet above sea level, and the 300-mile flight should take about twelve hours. Kavanagh will manufacture two 350,000-cubic-foot balloons, and for the expected −30-degree Celsius temperatures the open baskets will be lined to reduced wind chill.

At Machu Picchu the two crews will be transformed from fliers into rafters on the Urubamba, one of the wildest rivers in the world. The Urubamba rises from just north of Lake Titicaca and much of it has never been navigated; in places there is grade 6 white water, the worst grade possible. Dewhirst and company intend to raft down 800 miles of this river, past its confluence with the Ucayali in the lower regions of the Andes, until they arrive at Iquitos, the headwater of the great Amazon.

But the flying and the rafting may not be the most dangerous part of the expedition. Peru has an elected socialist government, but that doesn't suit all Peruvians. In the mountains and hills around Cuzco and Machu Picchu is based the Luminoscia, or Shining Path, an armed movement of left-wing Maoists who oppose the present government. Quite what they will think of two gaily coloured hot air balloons dropping out of the sky is one of the unknown factors of this expedition.

Another ballooning expedition, part of a four-year world-wide expedition, is also planned for South America. It is a French scientific expedition to the tropical rain forests of Brazil and Peru, the so-called 'lungs of the Earth'. This is the first stage of a three-part study of what's left of the world's equatorial forests, and began in mid-1989. The second stage is scheduled for October to December 1990 in South-East Asia, and the third stage for January to March 1992 in Africa, examining the three main equatorial regions of the world.

Following the success of the pilot study in French Guiana in 1986, the *Radeau des Cimes* hot air balloon of Gilles Ebersolt and Dany Cleyet-Marrel will be one of the vehicles for this extensive ecological study. A second lighter-than-air craft is also involved, a hot air

airship with an envelope of 265,000 cubic feet. This version of *le Radeau* will be used for transport and studies in the mountain forests, and incorporates a motor and a cabin for six people. The raft beneath, which will rest on the canopies of the forests, is similar to the hot air balloon's, with an area of 2,000 square feet.

◄ *Some members of the planned Andes expedition (left to right) Aden Wickes (in red), Brian Smith (obscured), Leo Dickinson and Chris Dewhirst.* Chris Dewhirst
► Le Radeau's *helium dirigible counterpart, designed for use in the mountainous forest areas.* Dany Cleyet-Marrel
▼ *The Incan city of Machu Picchu in the Peruvian Andes, half-way stage of the expedition from Nazca to Iquitos.* Bill Abbott (courtesy Chris Dewhirst)

▲ *The Great Wall of China — Changcheng — over which the Hong Kong club hopes to fly during the 1990s.* Chris Dewhirst

The scientific programme planned for these three expeditions is prodigious. It includes the study of oxygenation, gas concentrations, root systems, water systems, plant secretions, even genetics. The majority of this investigation will be conducted from the rafts beneath the balloon and airship by an international team of forty scientists.

The fruits of this programme will be studied and evaluated by the major universities and laboratories in France as well as their equivalents in Australia, Belgium, Great Britain, Luxembourg, India, Switzerland and the United States. Hopefully, by the time the expedition reaches Africa in 1992, there will still be some forest remaining for them to examine: at present an area of equatorial forest the size of Switzerland is being cut down every day.

The Hong Kong Balloon and Airship Club has hopes of more flying in the People's Republic of China in the next decade, over and around the Changcheng, the Great Wall, in the north of the country. As with many arrangements in China, this has all to be confirmed. The future of the Hong Kong club itself is in question. With the return of the British colony to China in 1997 pleasure flying may simply cease but, hopefully, in tandem with the agreed continuation of commercial flying, ballooning will also continue. The club's future seems promising because the People's Republic is now holding its own balloon meets, but after the tragedy of Tiananmen Square in June 1989 it is difficult to predict the future for Hong Kong.

The first international tournament in China was held in 1988, when hot air balloons from four countries gathered at the Air Sports School at Anyang, 370 miles south of Beijing. The Anyang International Hot Air Balloon Club is now established in this 3,000-year-old city, the first of the seven ancient capitals of China, and the school is the centre for pilot training and domestic competitions. China repeated the event in November 1989, immediately before the World Championships in Japan, and more balloonists from more countries were invited.

At the close of the 1980s Per Lindstrand of Britain began planning a hot air balloon attempt on Everest, the

▼ *The Himalayas, with Everest in the centre, goal of Per Lindstrand and Chris Bonington in* Star Flyer. *Leo Dickinson.(courtesy Chris Dewhirst)*

second such assault on this 29,028 foot mountain. His strategy will be to take off from east of Kathmandu in Nepal, ascend to about 33,000 feet and fly over Everest, or as close to it as possible, by riding the 100-knot jet stream winds. The landing is planned for Tibet after a four to six-hour flight and, with the support of the Chinese authorities, the ground team will retrieve the balloon there.

The 250,000-cubic-foot Thunder & Colt balloon has been christened *Star Flyer* after its major sponsor, Star Micronics UK Ltd, and it stands 91 feet high when fully inflated. With Lindstrand will be British mountaineer Chris Bonington, veteran of several Everest expeditions and leader of the first successful attempt on the southwest face in 1976. He is there as security in case *Star Flyer* is forced down in an inaccessible area of the Himalaya. The third member of the flight crew will be the cameraman, recording all for posterity. Training took place throughout 1989 in Europe, and included mountain climbing and survival courses on Mont Blanc.

A Japanese team attempted Everest during the first week of May 1990, but met with disaster when the balloon crashed and one crew member was hurt. Meanwhile, Lindstrand's team is on standby for October 1990.

Joe Kittinger of America also has a couple of ideas for the 1990s. One of these is to follow in the footsteps of

Salomon Andrée and attempt the North Pole by gas balloon. During his ill-fated flight of 1897 Andrée wrote in his diary: 'We are the first to travel here in a balloon. Will they consider us crazy, or follow our lead?' In 1989 Kittinger said: 'Andrée's proposed flight to the North Pole is feasible. The weather would allow it and the winds are right.'

The major problem that Andrée had with the *Eagle* in 1897 was that the intensely cold air had drastically reduced the amount of lift available from the hydrogen gas until, eventually, the balloon could no longer fly. Ice had also formed on the envelope. Helium gas presents the same problems, but a combined helium/hot air balloon would overcome them. The outer sleeve of hot air would keep the inner envelope of helium warm and so maintain its lift, and would also stop ice forming on the fabric. Perhaps in 1997 the first balloon will at last fly to the North Pole.

AROUND THE WORLD

Kittinger has also completed plans and logistics for the ultimate ballooning challenge — a non-stop around-the-world flight. He's now looking for backers for his gas balloon attempt. The first recorded balloon circumnavigation of the Earth was in 1966, by a small unmanned high-altitude balloon of the National Centre for Atmospheric Research of Colorado. Unmanned high-altitude balloons are now continually being launched with various scientific pay-loads for the study of upper air transportation systems, astro-physics and astronomy. Southampton University in Hampshire is one of the leaders in this field. In the 1970s it was the first to fly balloons from Britain to America — east to west across the Atlantic — using the jet streams. Contact with and control of these super-pressure balloons is maintained by radio links.

Non-stop orbits by these helium balloons are now the

rule rather than the exception; it was a shock when a recent meteorological balloon launched from Australia crashed in mountains in South America after only crossing the Pacific. The current record number of non-stop orbits of the Earth is thirty-three. And if unmanned balloons carrying a substantial pay-load can do it, why not manned balloons?

There have been several schemes put forward already and, since 1978, six unsuccessful attempts and two deaths. Some attempts never got off the ground, like the one from the Argentine in 1988 when the envelope was wrecked by strong ground winds during inflation. Americans Rowland Smith and John Petrehn had opted for a modern version of Pilâtre de Rozier's *Tour de Calais*, the combined gas and hot air balloon of 1785. The 1988 model stood 360 feet high, and incorporated a hot air balloon at the bottom and a helium balloon on top of that. A pressurised gondola was to take the two men on

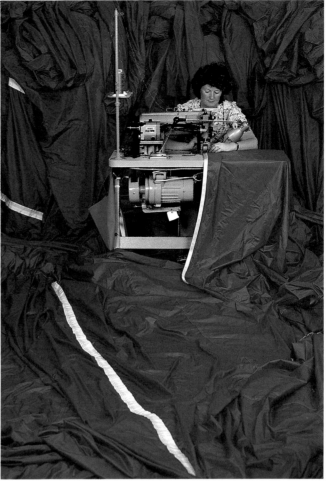

▲ *Meanwhile, the balloons for all these expeditions have to be made. Sewing a giant envelope* can seem a never-ending task.
Cameron Balloons
◄ *Ballooning across the Arctic pack ice to the North Pole is a lonely, dangerous business.* Dany Cleyet-Marrel
▼ *Weaving the traditional willow and cane basket. At Cameron Balloons much of this work is done by touch at the Royal Workshop for the Blind.* Cameron Balloons

161

their attempt to circumnavigate the southern hemisphere. They had chosen the town of Mendoza on the eastern slopes of the Andes for take-off, but strong winds and torrential rain be-devilled the launch and the attempt had to be aborted. The two men intend to try again.

One of the attempts more likely to have succeeded was that by Max Anderson and Don Ida of America in the early 1980s. They took off in the aptly named helium balloon *Jules Verne* from Luxor on the Nile, just south of the famed Valley of the Kings, and flew eastward from Egypt with the prevailing winds. They travelled nearly 3,000 miles across the Red Sea, Saudi Arabia, the Gulf of Oman and Pakistan before a small leak in the envelope forced them down at Hansi, in northern India. Their next obstacle was the Himalayas but, with the balloon persistently losing gas, Anderson and Ida had to land. Gas leakage forced Anderson down in two other around-the-world attempts.

Leaky envelopes have long been a problem in long range gas balloons. As the ambient air pressure decreases with height so the helium expands and exerts great pressure and stresses upon the envelope. The envelope can be vented to reduce the stress, but as the helium cools during the night it contracts, and loses its lifting capability, and the balloon descends. Eventually the balloon must land. A leaking envelope gives the same result. Super-pressure balloon envelopes are completely sealed, and the man-made fabric can withstand the pressure of the expanding helium.

Joe Kittinger will have to be quick in preparing for his around-the-world attempt, for there are rivals. One is Per Lindstrand, although his planned attempt will use a hot air balloon. This is not as crazy as it might at first seem. When he and Richard Branson touched down in Ireland after crossing the Atlantic in *Virgin Atlantic Flyer* they had used only a fifth of their fuel, and could conceivably have flown on across Russia. Lindstrand's plan is based upon his experiences in *Atlantic Flyer*, and will incorporate a combination of solar power supplemented by propane.

The Thunder & Colt balloon — provisionally called *Global Flyer* — will have an envelope capacity of 3.6 million cubic feet and will stand almost 230 feet high when fully inflated. It will be the largest hot air balloon ever built, and will be just 10 feet shorter than the Statue of Liberty. A laminated metalised envelope similar to *Atlantic Flyer*'s will be manufactured, but with one major change; 40 per cent of the fabric will be transparent. The weather patterns in the jet stream favour a winter flight, which, for the northern hemisphere, means an attempt between November and February. At this time of the year only 40 per cent of the day has direct sunlight above 30,000 feet. The transparent window of *Global Flyer* will be turned towards the sun by two electric motors rotating the balloon, so gaining the maximum effect of the solar energy. The capsule will be pressurised aircraft aluminium, large enough for a crew of three, and will include one sleeping berth. On top of the capsule and accessible through a hatch will be the high-altitude burners, pressurising engines and life support systems, while around the side will be slung disposable propane fuel tanks. Between 12 and 16 tons of liquid propane will be carried.

With Lindstrand will be a crew of two; Rory McCarthy and Mark Child of Britain, co-holders of the civilian free-fall parachute record and pilots both. McCarthy also holds the hang gliding altitude record of 36,700 feet. Two possible flight paths are currently being considered for this attempted circumnavigation.

The first, sub-tropical route lifts off from Texas and lies across the Atlantic, north Africa, northern India, southern China, and across the North Pacific Ocean back to North America, a distance of about 20,300 nautical miles. The jet stream weather should be stable, the wind speeds high, and this flight should take about 8½ days to complete. The second, polar route lifts off from Dakota and lies across the North Atlantic, southern Britain, central Europe, southern Russia, northern China, northern Japan, and across the far North Pacific back to North America, a distance of about 15,228 nautical miles. Although this flight path is almost 5,000 miles shorter — only an eight-day flight — the weather in these jet streams is less stable, and a probable three descents to about 10,000 feet would have to be made for course alterations. The final decision has not yet been made.

Full survival equipment will be carried in the capsule, but with careful planning and a touch of luck it won't be needed, and a hot air balloon should circumnavigate the Earth by 2000.

Meanwhile, a helium balloon attempt is already up and running. Using a super-pressure envelope and pressurised capsule, Julian Nott plans to circumnavigate the Earth in 1990. The balloon has been christened *Explorer*, and Nott's co-pilot for this record attempt is Buddy Squires of America. Built by Cameron Balloons, the double envelope has a capacity of 500,000 cubic feet and is completely sealed using gas-tight plastic. Around this is another layer to shield the main envelope from the sun. Fully inflated, *Explorer* stands 135 feet high. One of the problems of high-altitude flying in gas balloons is icing, causing weight increase and loss of performance. Nott and Squires will overcome this by flying *Explorer* above 30,000 feet like the unmanned research balloons; at that altitude the air is so cold that there is no moisture and hence no ice. The capsule, a design by Airship Industries of Britain developed from Nott's

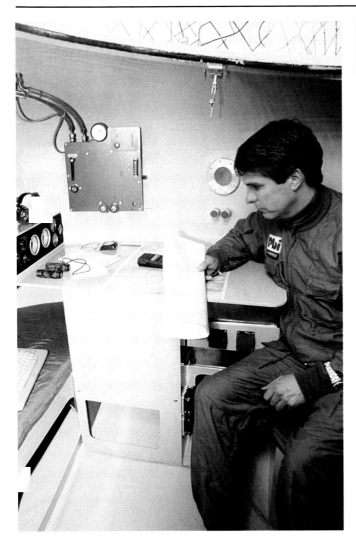

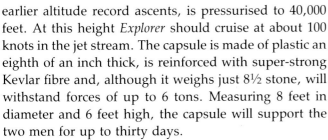

▲ *Early stages of the* Explorer *capsule, with Julian Nott inspecting one of the storage compartments. Two men will live in this space for about three weeks.* Schieffelin & Somerset (courtesy Julian Nott)
◄ *The* Explorer *capsule takes shape, while Julian Nott checks the console plans.* Julian Nott

earlier altitude record ascents, is pressurised to 40,000 feet. At this height *Explorer* should cruise at about 100 knots in the jet stream. The capsule is made of plastic an eighth of an inch thick, is reinforced with super-strong Kevlar fibre and, although it weighs just 8½ stone, will withstand forces of up to 6 tons. Measuring 8 feet in diameter and 6 feet high, the capsule will support the two men for up to thirty days.

This is one of the most carefully prepared balloon expeditions yet, based upon years of tests and experiments and a test flight of a prototype across Australia in 1984. Consultants include the Royal Air Force, the National Aeronautics and Space Administration, the National Centre for Atmospheric Research, and the Meteorological Office of Britain. An extensive programme of pollution investigation and atmospheric research will be carried out during the flight, and the information gained will be distributed internationally. Russia has also given permission for Nott to fly over its territory, a great help in deciding the take-off date and giving flexibility for choosing the flight paths. The expedition patrons are Sir Edmund Hillary and Thor Heyerdahl.

Explorer will take off from the United States Marine base at Tustin in California, from which Nott and Squires will ascend into the easterly moving upper jet stream. Their flight path will take the sub-tropical route across the United States to the North Atlantic Ocean, then over north Africa or southern Europe to the Middle East, over northern India or southern Russia, Indo-China and China, and then across the Pacific Ocean south of Japan and north of Hawaii to touch down in California again. It is estimated that the flight will take between fifteen and twenty days. Survival equipment including oxygen, parachutes, life rafts and automatic satellite beacons will also be carried on board.

Communications will be maintained throughout the attempt via satellite from a dish mounted on the capsule, and will include on-air interviews with radio stations, telephone links, and digitally generated live video links to anywhere in the world. About the only similarity between this attempt and that first gas balloon flight of 1783 by Charles and Robert is a bottle of champagne. Nott is taking a magnum of Möet on board *Explorer* to celebrate any outcome of the flight in the true tradition of ballooning.

Yet despite the obvious challenges of these expeditions they are, after all, only terrestrial flights. Ballooning on other planets in our solar system is the coming event for the 1990s.

EXTRA-TERRESTIAL

The Russian 1985 Vega mission to Venus, the closest planet to Earth, incorporated a ballooning experiment based on a concept by Professor Jacques Blaumont. Two research balloons were released from the orbiting satellite into the Venusian atmosphere with very successful results. A member of the French Academy of Sciences and advisor to CNES (National Space Agency of France), Blaumont sent further experimental ballooning equipment on the 1988 Russian probe to the Martian moon, Phobos. He now proposes an observation platform using a twin balloon — one helium and one solar envelope — for the 1992 Russsian mission to Mars.

The balloon will be released from the orbiting satellite by parachute and fly around the planet at between 3 and 5 miles above the surface, sending high resolution pictures back to Earth. At night the balloon will land and its pay-load will measure the chemical composition of the surface of Mars. A 'penetrator' on board will also attempt to dig through the oxidised top layer to the material beneath to determine its composition, and whether there are any organic remains.

The twin balloon has already been tested in France, and the principle was demonstrated to NASA in December 1987. The sealed helium envelope has a capacity of 70,600 cubic feet and is made of aluminiumised Kapton just 8 microns thick. The open solar envelope has a capacity of 134,200 cubic feet, and is made of black aluminiumised polyester on a textile frame.

During the Martian day the predominantly carbon dioxide atmosphere of the planet inside the solar envelope will be heated by the sun and the envelope will inflate. When a temperature difference of 50 degrees Celsius between the gas inside the envelope and the atmosphere gas is reached, the solar envelope will lift off, taking with it the neutrally buoyant helium envelope and the pay-load. At night, as the carbon dioxide cools, the solar envelope will gradually lose its lift and both envelopes will land. The helium envelope will have enough lift to remain upright so that its pay-load can operate, but be stable enough not to be disturbed by the gentle winds of the Martian night. Distances of about 300 miles would be covered each day, and Professor Blaumont estimates that the balloon should operate for at least ten Martian days (a Martian day is ten minutes longer than an Earth day).

If this concept is successful it will probably be used on the joint Russian/American mission planned for the late 1990s, in which samples of Mars will be brought back to Earth for analysis.

Heaven knows what the Martians will think when they see a Montgolfière and a Charlière flying over.

▲ *An artist's impression of the satellite delivery of the solar/helium balloon for the 1992 Russian Vega mission to Mars.* CNES/D. Ducros
▼ *How the balloon will land and take off during its flights around Mars.* CNES/D. Ducros

They are all gone into the world of light!
And I alone sit lingering here;
Their very memory is fair and bright,
and my sad thoughts doth clear.
                                    Henry Vaughan

Phil Castleton

Thom Roberts

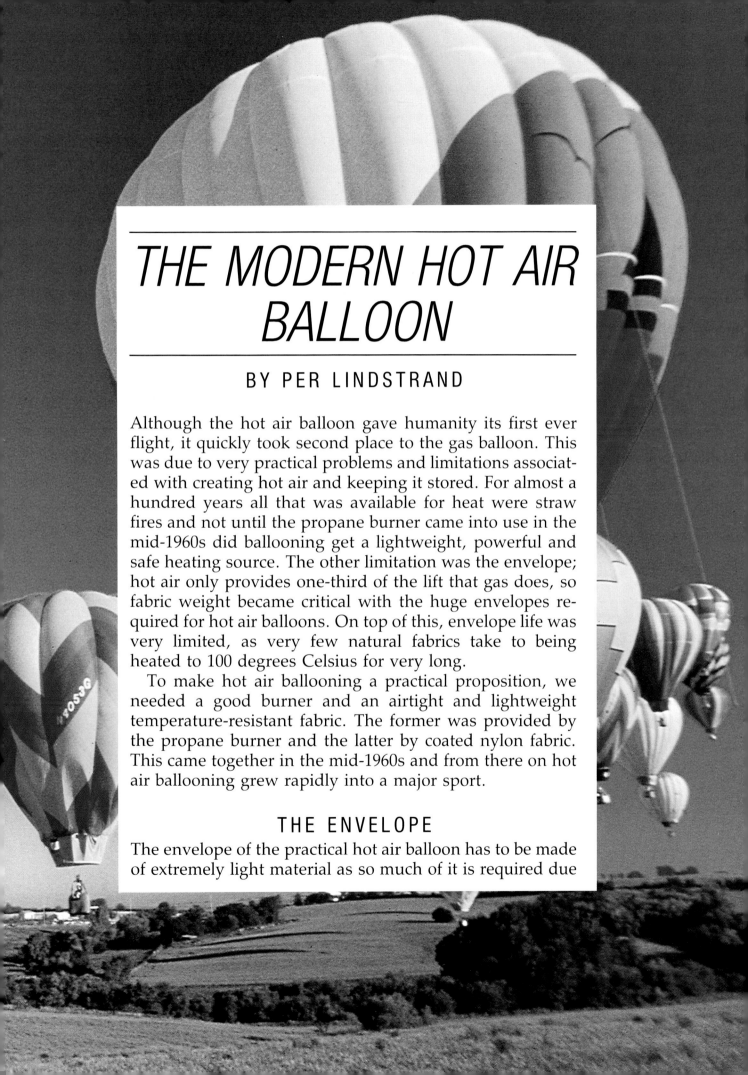

THE MODERN HOT AIR BALLOON

BY PER LINDSTRAND

Although the hot air balloon gave humanity its first ever flight, it quickly took second place to the gas balloon. This was due to very practical problems and limitations associated with creating hot air and keeping it stored. For almost a hundred years all that was available for heat were straw fires and not until the propane burner came into use in the mid-1960s did ballooning get a lightweight, powerful and safe heating source. The other limitation was the envelope; hot air only provides one-third of the lift that gas does, so fabric weight became critical with the huge envelopes required for hot air balloons. On top of this, envelope life was very limited, as very few natural fabrics take to being heated to 100 degrees Celsius for very long.

To make hot air ballooning a practical proposition, we needed a good burner and an airtight and lightweight temperature-resistant fabric. The former was provided by the propane burner and the latter by coated nylon fabric. This came together in the mid-1960s and from there on hot air ballooning grew rapidly into a major sport.

THE ENVELOPE

The envelope of the practical hot air balloon has to be made of extremely light material as so much of it is required due to the relatively small lifting capacity of heated air. As a general rule, a hot air balloon will lift a pound per 53 cubic feet which results in a typical 70,630-cubic-foot balloon if you want to fly four people for a couple of hours. This in turn means a surface area of about 1,080 square yards, which is a lot of fabric — more than half a mile, in fact. Not only need the fabric be very light, but it must also be soft and pliable so that it can be squashed into a small bag without undue crew effort and also without incurring damage to itself such as cracks or creases.

However, it has to be airtight and possess sufficient strength to carry the pay-load. The last two properties tend to go hand in hand, in that a fabric that is strong enough to safely carry the load is usually sufficiently airtight. Likewise, both properties tend to deteriorate in parallel, making the balloon wear out structurally at the same time as it starts losing air.

Apart from the very early balloons, all balloon fabric is now coated with either polyurethane or some sort of silicone/elastomer. The weight relationship between fabric and coating is usually about 2:1 and nylon is the favoured fibre, although polyester is occasionally used. Generally, nylon is stronger than polyester for the same weight, but polyester tends to be more ultra-violet resistant and often has better colour fastness. Today, 80 per cent of the world's balloons are made from nylon fabric, and although nylon may appear to be an old fibre compared with modern developments such as Kevlar, it does have very safe and predictable behaviour. This cannot be said for the modern high-tech fibres, which also have a poor ultra-violet resistance. Dependability and a known wear pattern are very important in ballooning, as balloons rarely get the attention other aircraft do and often operate in an environment well away from proper maintenance facilities. The life of a hot air balloon envelope is relatively short compared with the rest of the craft, but this is understandable if you consider that the fabric is exposed to strong sunlight while maintaining 100 degrees Celsius. By relatively short, we mean on the average 6 years, which is quite sufficient for normal applications. Any lengthening of this period would necessitate using a heavy material and therefore would result in a clumsy balloon or a further developed material and a much higher cost. Both these alternatives are open to the balloon buyer, but normally only a fare-paying passenger operation is prepared to pay the financial penalty of a much longer-lasting fabric. The future will probably see the development of a lighter fabric while maintaining the current strength and life for the private operator, who is more concerned with ease of packing than ultimate life; the commercial full-time operator will accept the current heavy fabrics being developed for longer life.

Two kinds of deflation system remain today, developed from a host of early inventions: the parachute valve and velcro rip. The parachute valve is re-sealable and therefore re-usable, ultra-safe and fitted to almost all small and medium-sized balloons. For large balloons, where the required surface area of a parachute valve would limit its size, one usually finds a velcro rip which can dump more quickly, but it is not resealable and is a once only valve used for landing. It is not as trouble-free as a parachute valve, but it has been perfected into a safe and predictable deflation mechanism.

THE BURNER AND FUEL SYSTEMS

Our typical four-passenger hot air balloon requires about 800 megajoules per hour of heat input to fly and this, in more understandable terms, is 10 pounds of propane. By experience we have found that it is a lot easier to fly a balloon with a much oversized burner used intermittently than by adjusting a constant burner. The former alternative is also more comfortable in that you get long spells of silence between short spells of burner noise. Today's burner has an output of 2 megawatts and we would use the burner for 11 per cent of the time.

Propane is the universally accepted fuel for hot air balloons for very simple reasons; it can be stored in sealed bottles as a liquid, and kept at its normal vapour pressure at a typical 100 psi while vaporising instantly when released into free air. This means that one can build a very simple and high output burner using no pumps, the natural vapour pressure being sufficient to force the fuel out to the burner from the cylinders. By using a straightforward vaporising coil exposed in the main flame, large quantities of fuel can be vaporised and burnt, which would require elaborate combustion chambers if, for example, petrol, diesel or kerosene was used. The energy level in propane is virtually the same as that in other hydrocarbons such as petrol, and the only other hydrocarbons with similar physical properties would be butane and ethane, butane being on the low side as regards vapour pressure, while ethane is on the high side. Butane is used in hot climates where propane is deemed a bit risky due to high vapour pressure. Ethane is only used as a vapour pressure booster for flying in very cold climates. The only disadvantage with propane is that the cylinders must be built as pressure vessels, being able to withstand an ultimate pressure of about 300 psi, which results in a weight penalty of about 25 per cent over that of the weight of fuel. On the other hand, it eliminates pumps and energy sources to drive the pumps, so on the whole it represents a gain. The only time non-pressurised fuel is used is for long record-breaking flights where paraffin burners have been used to avoid the weight of heavy tanks.

▲ *In the darkness of the early morning the large envelope is inflated.*
Thunder & Colt Balloons

The burner can be broken down into the following components:

vaporising coil
on/off valve
pressure gauges
pilot light
igniter.

The vaporising coil takes the raw liquid propane and circulates it through the coil that is located around the main flame. The coil itself is made from a heat-resistant stainless steel such as Inconel and, of course, as the flow is only operated intermittently, a good quality on/off valve is required. The pilot light is on all the time and is fed either via a separate vapour hose from the top of the fuel cylinder or off a liquid source tapped into the main burner supply, carrying its own vaporiser. Propane will only combust as a gas, so any liquid fuel would have to be vaporised before combustion.

The balloon burner is usually manufactured from high-grade stainless steel and aluminium and has an almost indefinite life apart from rubber seals, gaskets and other plastic materials, which are replaced on an on-condition basis. Therefore, burners are only replaced as they become obsolete in performance or noise level and the latter is becoming more and more important as more balloons fly over the same land. Strangely enough, animals in nature seem completely unaffected by balloons, something that is very evident as aerial photo safaris in Africa are almost always conducted by balloon. Tame animals scare more easily and often object to low-flying balloons. The remedy is quiet burners and there has been considerable development to answer this need, particularly of so-called liquid fire burners. These burners are less efficient than the vaporising coil type; they not only lower the noise considerably but also change the noise spectra, which appears equally important. For commercial balloon operators the liquid fire burner is a must, but it is only fitted in conjunction with a standard burner as it is also less precise in its flame pattern. Burners tend to be produced in modular sizes, and for increased burner power one adds more modules rather than a bigger burner. The single burner module is thus designed to operate underneath the small-sized balloon such as a 42 or 56; a twin unit is normally fitted to size 77 and 105; while a triple unit or a quadruple unit is fitted to balloons over size 120.

Today's balloonist can have all the burner power he or she needs by simply increasing the number of modules on the balloon, the limitation being premature wear on the balloon by overheating. The future development of burners will be directed towards lowering their noise level in order to maintain good neighbour relations.

INTERNATIONAL COMPETITION TASKS

Judge Declared Goal The competition judges decide upon the goal, and the pilot must take off from the launch area and drop a marker as close to this goal as possible.

Pilot Declared Goal The pilot declares the goal before the competition, and must take off from the launch area and drop a marker as close to this goal as possible.

Hesitation Waltz The pilot takes off from the launch area and attempts to drop markers as close as possible to several judge declared goals.

Hare and Hounds A 'hare' balloon pilot takes off from the launch area, lands somewhere, and displays a marker up-wind of the basket. The other pilots, the 'hounds', take off from the launch area and must drop their marker as close as possible to the 'hare' marker.

Fly-in The competition judges declare a goal and pilots must choose their own launch area from which to take off and drop their marker on the goal.

Thom Roberts

Fly-on This is a supplementary task where a pilot declares a second goal to which he or she must fly after dropping a marker at the first goal.

Elbow A pilot attempts to achieve the greatest change in direction of the balloon in flight as possible.

Watership Down Pilots must choose their own launch areas, take off and fly to another launch area from which a 'hare' balloon will take off at a certain time. The pilot must then chase the 'hare' balloon, as in a hare and hounds.

Race to a Line A pilot must fly to cross a decreed line in the fastest time after taking off from a common launch area.

The Gordon Bennett Memorial The pilots attempt to drop their markers as close as possible to a set goal: this is for gas balloons.

The Gordon Bennett Trophy The pilots attempt to fly the greatest distance possible from a common launch area: this is for gas balloons.

Ribbon Race Two balloons are tied together by a length of ribbon about 100 to 200 feet long. The pilots take off together and fly for as long as possible without breaking the ribbon, the winners being the two who keep the ribbon intact for the longest time. Some pilots have managed more than two hours.

Splash and Dash The pilot has to fly the balloon over a lake or pond or river and touch the surface of the water with the basket. The winner is the pilot who makes the most touches in a given amount of time, usually with a required 30 to 60-second time gap between splashes.

Thom Roberts

BIBLIOGRAPHY

Hayes, Will, *Balloon Digest*, Hayes, Santa Barbara, California, 1985.

Jackson, Donald, *The Aeronauts*, Time-Life Books, Virginia, 1981.

Luck, Peter, *A Time to Remember*, William Heinemann, Australia, 1988.

National Geographic, volume 164, nos 2, 6, National Geographic Society, Washington, DC, 1983 and 1985.

Nørgaard, Eric, *The Book of Balloons*, Lademann Publishing House, Inc., Copenhagen, 1970.

Reynaud, Marie-Hélène, *Les Frères Montgolfier*, Les Montgolfier et Vidalon, Annonay, 1981.

Sinclair, Kevin, *Over China*, Intercontinental Publishing Corporation Ltd, Hong Kong/China Great Wall Publishing House, Beijing, 1988.

Virgin Atlantic Airways, *Virgin Atlantic Flyer*, Crawley, Sussex, 1987.

Wirth, Dick and Jerry Young, *Ballooning*, Orbis Publishing, London, 1980.

Botting, Douglas, *The Giant Airships*, Time-Life, Alexandria, Virginia, 1981.

Allen, Peter, *The 91 Before Lindbergh*, Airlife Publishing Ltd, Shrewsbury, England, 1984.

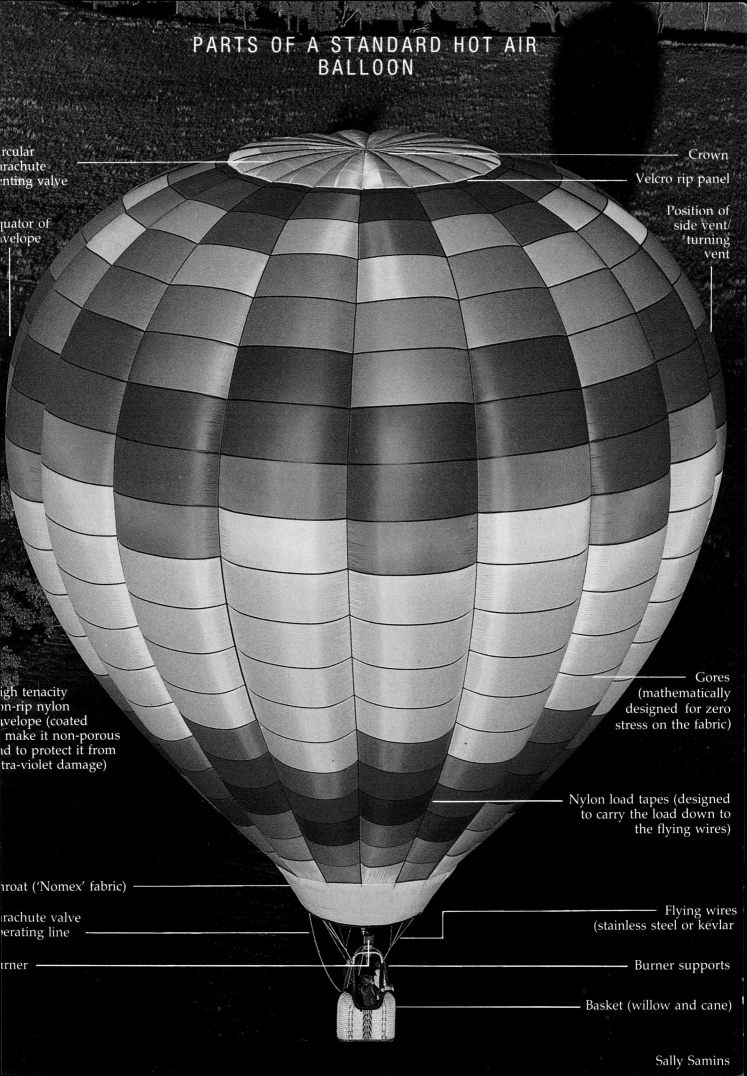

PARTS OF A STANDARD HOT AIR BALLOON

Circular parachute venting valve

Crown

Velcro rip panel

Equator of envelope

Position of side vent/ turning vent

High tenacity non-rip nylon envelope (coated to make it non-porous and to protect it from ultra-violet damage)

Gores (mathematically designed for zero stress on the fabric)

Nylon load tapes (designed to carry the load down to the flying wires)

Throat ('Nomex' fabric)

Parachute valve operating line

Flying wires (stainless steel or kevlar

Burner

Burner supports

Basket (willow and cane)

Sally Samins

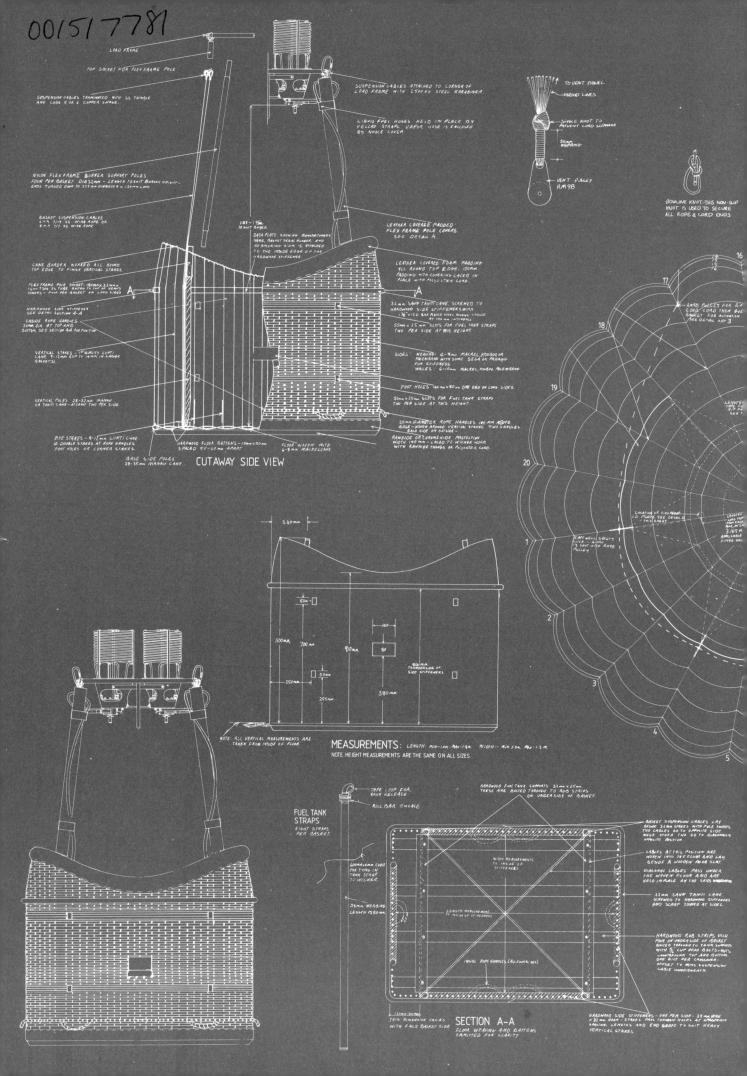

001517781